ONE MORE VALLEY, ONE MORE HILL

The Story of Aunt Clara Brown

ONE MORE VALLEY, ONE MORE HILL

The Story of Aunt Clara Brown

LINDA LOWERY

Landmark Books

Random House New York

Copyright © 2002 by Fudrick and Friends, Inc.

Introduction copyright © 2002 by Patricia C. McKissack.

All rights reserved under International and Pan-American Copyright Conventions. Published in the United States by Random House Children's Books, a division of Random House, Inc., New York, and simultaneously in Canada by Random House of Canada Limited, Toronto.

www.randomhouse.com/kids

Library of Congress Cataloging-in-Publication Data

Lowery, Linda.

One more valley, one more hill : the story of Aunt Clara Brown / Linda Lowery.

p. cm. — (Landmark books)

SUMMARY: Chronicles the life of the woman called Aunt Clara Brown, who was born into slavery and became a pioneer and entrepreneur, earning money to bring other former slaves to a new start in Colorado. Includes bibliographical references and index.

ISBN 0-375-81092-7 (trade) — ISBN 0-375-91092-1 (lib. bdg.) — ISBN 0-375-81093-5 (pbk.)

1. Brown, Clara, 1800–1885—Juvenile literature. 2. African American women pioneers—Colorado—Biography—Juvenile literature. 3. Women pioneers—Colorado—Biography—Juvenile literature.

4. Free African Americans—Colorado—Biography—Juvenile literature. 5. Frontier and pioneer life—Colorado—Juvenile literature. 6. Central City (Colo.)—Biography—Juvenile literature.

[1. Brown, Clara, 1800–1885. 2. African Americans—Biography. 3. Women—Biography. 4. Frontier and pioneer life—Colorado. 5. Colorado—History—To 1876.] I. Title.

F785.N4 L695 2002   978.8'00496073'0092—dc21   2002002845

Printed in the United States of America   First Edition   10 9 8 7 6 5 4 3 2 1

RANDOM HOUSE and colophon and LANDMARK BOOKS and colophon are registered trademarks of Random House, Inc.

To all young people whose ancestors overcame impossible odds: May you be inspired to write and paint and dance the stories that are in your bones.

Contents

ONE MORE VALLEY, ONE MORE HILL

The Story of Aunt Clara Brown

Introduction

During the 1950s, when I was growing up in Tennessee and Missouri, I loved history and read lots of books about great American heroes—Thomas Jefferson, Benjamin Franklin, Paul Revere, John Adams, and others. All white men.

As I grew older, I started wondering, Didn't women and people of color do anything worth writing a book about? There were so few, if any, stories in my textbooks about African Americans. We were an invisible people. So I assumed women and blacks hadn't made any significant contributions to our nation.

Nothing could have been more untrue.

For me, American history is like a big puzzle, and every person, place, and event is a puzzle piece. For years, the African Americans' and women's pieces were missing. That meant I never saw a picture of history that was clear or complete. As a young reader searching, as a teacher trying to inspire, and as a writer telling a story, I have sought out those pieces of history that have been marginalized or minimized, or forgotten entirely by mainstream texts. By sharing stories and more stories about *all* who helped shape this country, the puzzle picture becomes brighter, more colorful, more honest, and much more interesting.

This book is a wonderful discovery, a new puzzle piece for the great American picture.

Books such as this remind us how important it is to celebrate our diverse ethnic heritage. In the past three decades, I have seen a number of books published about men and women who deserve recognition—Frederick Douglass, Carter G. Woodson, W.E.B. DuBois, Harriet Tubman, Sojourner Truth, Rosa Parks, Fannie Lou Hamer, and the Reverend Dr. Martin Luther King, Jr. But there are countless others who are waiting for their stories to be told.

Aunt Clara Brown is just such a person.

Many readers may not be familiar with Clara Brown. Linda Lowery has done an excellent job of bringing her to life in this well-written, highly dramatic page-turner. Get ready to be mesmerized by Aunt Clara, an intrepid woman who lived a life of triumph mixed with devastating loss and pain. Born a slave, Clara knew the horror of having her child and her husband sold away from her, never to be seen again. But the suffering she endured strengthened her for the journey that lay ahead. Lowery follows Clara through a young America just on the edge of wilderness. With only her faith in God and herself,

Clara faced the unknown. Was she afraid? Yes. But she was brave enough to take the first step, and smart enough to keep going.

In Virginia, in the bloody fields of pre–Civil War Kansas, and in Colorado, where she became an entrepreneur and a philanthropist, Aunt Clara lived the life of a classic American hero.

The *Denver Tribune-Republican* stated in an 1885 tribute: "We hold in grateful remembrance the kind old friend . . . who, rising from the humble position of a slave to the angelic type of noble woman, won our sympathy and commanded our respect." Words like these were not often used to describe black women. But Aunt Clara Brown transcended both gender and race to touch the hearts of all who knew her. My wish is that young readers everywhere will embrace Clara's story and, in so doing, add another piece to the puzzle that is our American history.

Patricia C. McKissack
Chesterfield, Missouri

Author's Note

In writing this book, I had to make a sensitive decision about language. Would I use modern terms when referring to Native Americans, African Americans, and multi-ethnic Americans? Or would I use words like *Indian, Negro,* and *mulatto,* which were typical of Clara's nineteenth-century America?

The terms used back then have connotations now that can be extremely negative. When I attempted to use contemporary language, however, I encountered two problems. First, the modern words were just that—modern. In the context of a narrative about the past, they seemed jarring and out of place. But second, and more importantly, the modern terms suggested a racial tolerance and respect that rarely existed in Clara's time.

With that in mind, I have decided to use the nineteenth-century language. I hope that, as uncomfortable as we are with them today, thcsc words will serve as a reminder of the world Clara lived in.

CHAPTER 1

Wilderness Home

By the time Clara Brown was ten, she could bake a pie, darn a sock, mend a hole in a shoe, and launder and press a fine Sunday shirt. She could also pluck the feathers off a chicken, and heal a sick farmhand with nothing but a handful of plants.

However, she couldn't tell you when to celebrate her birthday, or even exactly how old she was. Nobody had bothered to register her birth, because Clara Brown was born a slave. To their owners, slaves were not important enough to be given birth certificates—or to be given last names. The baby-girl slave, born just after the turn of the nineteenth century, was simply called "Clara."

Based on Clara's fuzzy memories, she was probably born in January of 1800, in slaves' quarters in Spotsylvania County, Virginia. Three years later, little Clara was sold with her mother to a farmer named Ambrose Smith of Fredericksburg, Virginia.

She remembered her tiny hands grasping the folds in her mammy's cotton skirts, and the sound of a pounding gavel, and loud yelling voices. That day, Clara's papa and her older brothers and sisters were all sold to different owners. She was not old enough to remember them, and she would never see them again.

Clara's first clear memories began in 1809, the year

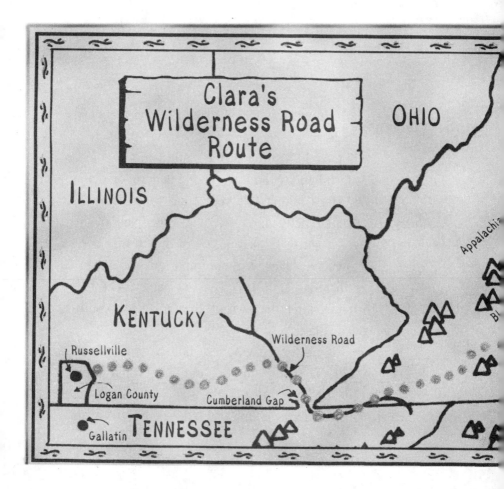

Abraham Lincoln was born. That year, the Smith family moved west. Back then, "west" meant moving to Kentucky or to Tennessee, a wilderness of woods, bears, and Indians, with a sprinkling of fledgling pioneer towns. Ambrose and Myra Smith packed up their three children and their slaves, including Clara and her mother, and headed from Virginia to the wilds of Kentucky. They planned to put down roots in the country, outside a small town called Russellville. They traveled with five other families by covered wagon over the "Wilderness Road." An awesome and treacherous trek, it was Clara's first taste of pioneering.

The Wilderness Road had been hand-chopped, cut with axes through the Appalachian Mountains by Daniel Boone and his men back in 1775. It snaked through the Cumberland Gap, a trail full of boulders and narrow rock passageways. Clara's pioneering party had to ford rivers, climb mountains, and cross hostile Indian territory.

River crossings were a huge task: the horses were

unhitched and forced to swim—which they hated. When the water was too deep to walk through, rafts were built on the riverbank to float the people and the wagons across. Trudging up a mountain was no easy chore, either. The wagons were so heavily loaded that the horses couldn't possibly haul them uphill. Men looped thick ropes around tree trunks higher up on the mountain and tied them to the wagons. Several men then planted themselves up above and, using the trees for leverage, pulled on the ropes to give the horses extra help. The strain was so great that the ropes dug into the trees, often leaving deep gashes in the trunks—gashes so deep that they would still be visible 150 years later.

Clara remembered wagons breaking, falling apart, and being left behind in pieces. She saw horses shot because their legs had been broken. She saw people die, and watched as they were hurriedly buried beside the road. Epitaphs were scratched onto scrap wood that was pounded in for headstones.

The "far west" land belonged not to the white settlers, but to the Algonquin, Delaware, Shawnee, and other Indian tribes. They were startled and outraged that their hunting land was suddenly being invaded, and they sometimes attacked. Unlike the white pioneers, Clara and her mother never felt threatened by these Indians. Clara's grandmother had been full-blooded Cherokee, so her mother was half-Cherokee and Clara was one-quarter Cherokee.

Years later, Clara told a reporter: "You see, I'm part Indian myself, honey, and even if I wasn't, why, I'd never have been afraid of them." Trusting and innocent, Clara and her mother did not know that most Indians treated Negro and white pioneers—as well as Indians from other tribes—with the same wariness. To them, all settlers were invaders, no matter what the color of their skin. Luckily, the Smith party made the crossing with no dangerous confrontations.

When the wagons pulled into Logan County, Kentucky, in May of 1809, there was nothing there but raw land. It was beautiful, with lush green hills, flowering trees, and Big Muddy Creek, a babbling stream, running clear through.

Clara's mother got busy helping Mrs. Smith with cooking, laundering, and milking the cows. The men's jobs were to put up houses, haul the rocks and boulders from the pastures, and plant tobacco while the season was ripe. The land, however, had to be cultivated before the men could plant.

Clara helped. Along with the two Smith boys, eleven-year-old Matt and nine-year-old Jeremy, she dragged branches into ditches, stacking them high. The branches were left sitting in huge piles until they got "buggy"—a pioneer term for bug-infested. Then the men set them ablaze, sending billows of smoke into the skies. When the fires went out, the remaining mounds of ashes were three times as tall as Clara. The field hands then turned the ashes, with the dead bugs inside, into the soil for fertilizer.

Before long, there was a fine new farm. The Smiths' slaves had built the "big house" for the master's family, some barns, cabins for the slaves, and a milk-house over the creek so the dairy products would stay cool. Life felt stable and secure again for Clara. She and her mammy settled with other "house Negroes" in a slaves' cabin that had a floor—not of dirt, but nice wooden boards.

They handled duties for Mistress Smith inside the big house. On laundry day, they filled wooden tubs with soap shavings and used a washboard to scrub the dirt from the clothes and linens. After the laundry was rinsed and dried on the line, they heated a heavy iron on the stove and pressed out the wrinkles till everything was nice and flat. When rugs needed cleaning, Clara helped haul them outside to hang over poles. Her mother showed her how to beat the dust out of them with an iron rod.

Clara learned to darn, weaving threads through holes in shirts and trousers and socks to mend them. She gathered eggs from the hens, and if they weren't laying, tucked other eggs into their nests to encourage them to produce more. She learned to use an axe to cut off a chicken's head on the chopping block. She learned to prepare the chicken for a tasty supper: roasted, or fried, or boiled in a hearty stew, with fresh vegetables from the garden or dandelion leaves from the fields.

When autumn came and the leaves turned fiery bright, Clara's mammy taught her to pickle and dry and preserve foods, so they could use them all winter for cooking. Clara gathered herbs and hung them in bunches to dry. She made blueberry and apple and cherry preserves and stored them in jars. She packed meat in barrels of rock salt. She stored the parsnips and turnips and sweet potatoes in the dark root cellar, where they would last.

Mrs. Smith saw that Clara was a bright girl, always curious and helpful. So in quiet moments, she taught Clara how to read and write. In most states, there were laws that meant jail time if an owner was caught educating a slave. Education meant power, and power meant that slaves might get "uppity notions" about wanting to be free. But Kentucky's laws were not so strict. As long as she kept only to the basics, and did not teach materials that could incite "insurrection," Mrs. Smith was free to educate Clara.

On Sundays, the Smiths would dress up and take Clara and her mother to the Methodist chapel. This was no white church with stained-glass windows, the kind to be found in nearby Russellville. Instead, a preacher named Valentine Cook had a school and a chapel right on his farm, and local people gathered there for Sunday services. Slaves could worship in the church, but they had to sit in a separate "colored" gallery in the rear.

Although Clara did not know it at the time, churchgoing was not a common experience for slaves. More often than not, the master went to church on Sundays, leaving his slaves behind to congregate in the yard for worship. An overseer would read to them from the Bible, choosing passages that reminded the slaves of their subservient roles, such as: "Servants, obey your masters." Many slaves never knew that the Bible contained any messages of joy or hope or equality.

But it wasn't that way for Clara. She was surrounded by people of great faith. Her mother and her masters always made sure she attended church and special religious celebrations. From an early age, she learned that the Bible was filled with uplifting messages. Many years later, when she was in her eighties, she remembered what she called the most important moment of her life.

It was 1810, and the Smiths took Clara and her mother to a huge revival meeting on the Muddy River, where people trekked in from all over Kentucky to pray. They recited passages from the Bible. They sang songs to give hope to the downhearted, and offer forgiveness for sinners. A preacher's voice boomed, rattling the tent poles.

This event was a once-in-a-lifetime experience for Clara, who had an "awakening" there. She felt that the spirit of God spoke to her. He promised to guide and protect her always. When she was older, Clara talked about the importance her faith played in her life from the time she was ten.

"Lordy me, darlin'," she said, "I was nothing but a child when God came to me and took me to Jesus." This spiritual foundation, this unshakable faith, kept Clara steady and hopeful when life's trials challenged her body and soul.

From that week on, Clara believed that, no matter how grim, how tortured, or how unbearable her life might sometimes seem, God would "bear her up" and see her through.

Pioneer Sayings

Uppity—*In Clara's day, wheat flour was considered better (and was more expensive) than flour made from rye or oats. When a mistress gave a fancy dinner party, she would ask the cook to make the top crust of a pie from wheat flour, so that her guests would be impressed, even if the bottom crust was baked with a cheaper flour. The terms "upper crust" and "uppity" came to mean someone who acted fancy or rich.*

Like a Chicken with Its Head Cut Off—*The nervous system of a chicken doesn't die immediately when the bird's head is chopped off. Often, the headless body can still race around for a few minutes. Clara would certainly have seen an occasional headless chicken running around in wild circles on the Smith farm. When a person acted distracted, trying to do too many things at once, pioneers would say: "He's running around like a chicken with its head cut off!"*

Nest Egg—*To encourage hens to lay a lot of eggs, farmers often left one egg in the nest. Sometimes it was a real egg, and sometimes it was made of clay or wood. A nest egg came to mean a bit of money saved for the future: a sum invested to produce more money.*

Revivals

In the early 1800s, it was very common for pioneer preachers to travel through Kentucky and other states, holding Christian prayer meetings. People camped out overnight, sometimes for a week at a time, and spent the days praying, singing, and listening to ministers preach. Hundreds of thousands of people had "awakenings," turned "from their wicked ways," and converted to Christianity as a result of these revivals.

CHAPTER 2

Jumping the Broom

When Clara was eighteen, Matt Smith left for Transylvania College, and his father needed someone to take over his share of the work. Master Smith bought a new slave, a strong, handsome farmhand and carpenter named Richard.

When Richard looked at Clara, he saw a tall girl with Cherokee cheekbones and skin as brown as burnt sugar. Clara had an easy, deep laugh and a great big heart—anybody could see that in her shining black eyes. Richard smiled in an extra-friendly way. He was smitten.

That very year, 1818, Richard asked Clara to marry him. Clara said yes. But first they had to ask Master Smith for official permission. He not only consented, but he and his wife planned a joyous wedding feast. Slaves from all the neighboring farms were invited to witness as Clara and Richard jumped over the broom to their place of marriage. They celebrated into

A typical slave quarters on a Southern plantation. Most were overcrowded, uncomfortable, and disease-ridden.

the night with singing and dancing under the soft Kentucky stars.

Richard and Clara were very happy. Unlike slaves on many other plantations, they lived together in the same cabin, with Clara's mother and other house Negroes. Clara and her mammy kept life in the big house running smoothly. In the slow, hot summers, when the Kentucky hills were a rich blue-green and horses trotted playfully across sunlit meadows, they baked fresh berry pies, topped with cream from the family cows. When the oak and chestnut leaves turned blazing red and yellow, they salted meats and dried mint and parsley. In winter, they prepared kettles full of soup and put candles made of beeswax on the Christmas tree. Spring meant they would clean the house, top to bottom, and hang the laundry outside to dry in the breeze.

Those same springs and summers, Richard joined the other slaves in the field, planting, fertilizing, and cultivating. A wise farmer scheduled his planting according to the power of the moon phases, and often used *The Old Farmer's Almanac.* Under Master Smith's guidance, Richard and the other farm-hands sowed tobacco seeds when the moon was waxing and cultivated when the moon was waning. Their busiest time was at the harvest, when the wide leaves were cut and dried in the sun.

But Richard's main job was carpentry. He could do anything he turned his hand to—fixing leaky roofs, rotting barns, or wobbly furniture. Sometimes Ambrose Smith contracted him out to build houses for local farmers.

Richard, Clara, and her mother knew very well that they were blessed to have kind owners. Certainly, Ambrose and Myra Smith were strict. Like all slave owners, they expected absolute obedience from their slaves. If house slaves were slovenly or impolite, they would be banned from the big house and put to work in the fields. The Smiths named all the new slave babies themselves, since they were considered property. But they did not work their slaves to death or stage public whippings and hangings.

In 1820, Clara and Richard had their first child, Richard Jr. By 1826, Richard and Clara had had three more children: Margaret, and her twin sisters, Eliza Jane and Paulina Ann. The children helped out with farm work in the very same fields Clara had when she was young. When their chores were finished, they scrambled around in the pastures and dangled their feet in Big Muddy Creek.

Then one summer day in 1834, when the twins were eight years old, Clara's life took a tragic turn. Paulina Ann went for a dip in the creek. Suddenly, the water rushed around her and dragged her downstream. Eliza Jane saw Paulina flapping her arms, struggling to stay afloat. She bobbed to the surface, only to be drawn down again.

Eliza Jane raced to the big house, screaming for help. Clara dashed from her ironing and grabbed the dinner bell, ringing it as hard as she could so the men in the fields would hear the alarm. Then grasping tight to 'Liza Jane's hand, she bolted to the creek. There was no sign of Paulina Ann.

Men and women came hurrying from their work in the fields. Richard dove into the water, searching through the weeds. When he finally rose up, he was holding the body of his little girl, limp in his arms. Paulina Ann had gotten tangled in the weeds at the bottom of the stream. She was dead.

Devastated, Clara sat in the darkness of the slaves' cabin, wailing and rocking by the fire. She did not know how to heal her pain. One night, she knelt on the wood floor and began praying out loud. "Ask and it shall be given to you," the Bible told her. She asked for peace. Once again, as at the revival, Clara felt God comforting her, bringing her the solace she so needed.

From then on, Clara dropped to her knees and prayed aloud whenever the spirit moved her. It made no difference where she was or who was watching. She needed a word with the Lord, and that was that.

"Uncle" Butler, a preacher slave from another farm, came to perform the burial services. Usually, slaves were not allowed to be buried in white cemeteries. But Clara, her mother, and Richard were like family to the Smiths. Paulina Ann was laid to rest beneath a mulberry tree in the family cemetery.

Eliza Jane sobbed through the ceremony and sobbed for days after. She could not stop blaming herself for her twin sister's death. The happy-go-lucky little girl who had played in the fields and swam cool as a fish in the creek was gone. Night after night, 'Liza awoke screaming in terror. Her legs kept jittering, her hands rubbed together nonstop. She was always feeling sick to her stomach. Her parents held her and rocked her and sang to her, but nothing seemed to calm her down.

People began to talk, saying that Eliza Jane had gone plumb crazy. Clara knew better. It would take time for her little girl to heal. She needed her mammy to see her through this troubled time. And Clara vowed to be there to comfort 'Liza Jane forever.

But forever was not something you could count on, if

you were a slave. For Clara and Eliza Jane, forever turned out to be less than two years.

Slave Marriages

Slaves couldn't legally marry, since they were not considered citizens. Instead, with the master's permission, they created their own wedding ceremonies. A man and woman stood before witnesses, pledged their love to each other, and then, holding hands, they literally jumped over a broom on the ground.

For many African peoples, a broom symbolized homemaking, two people creating a home and family together. It meant they were sweeping away their past lives and jumping into their new life of marriage. Slaves in America used that symbol to begin a new tradition.

Here are some lines from an old "broom-jumping" song called "At an Ole Virginia Wedding":
"Let none but Him that makes the thunder
Put this he-male and this she-male asunder.
The broomstick's jumped, the world's not wide.
She's now your own, salute your bride."

CHAPTER 3

Summer Tears

It was summertime, 1836. The past two years had been hard on Clara and her family. First, her mother had died, just a few months after Paulina Ann. Then Ambrose Smith had passed on. It was a struggle for his family to keep up the cost of running the farm. After several months of cutting back expenses, they realized it was impossible. The Smiths were forced to sell most of their property, including their slaves.

Now it was County Court Day, always a hot summer day of celebration in Russellville. Farmers from all over Logan County gathered to buy and sell. Vendors shouted, hawking their wares. There were kitchen utensils and farm tools piled on tables, anything and everything needed to run a farm: milk buckets, branding irons, harnesses, sledgehammers, tin washboards. There were spreads of home-baked pies and jugs of lemonade. There was fiddle music and dancing.

An engraving from an 1856 issue of *The Illustrated London News* depicts a young woman on the block at a Richmond, Virginia, slave auction. Prospective buyers look her over casually.

Up front was a low wooden platform, the auction block, where auctioneers were hired to sell people's goods at the highest price they could get: furniture, old family scrapbooks, wheelbarrows, wagons, cattle . . . and slaves. That day, about thirty slaves were up for sale. Clara's whole family was among them.

As people milled around beneath the scorching summer sun, sipping their lemonade and twirling their parasols, Clara stood silently beside Richard and her children. This was the day she had prayed would never come, a day like the one in 1803, when Clara's papa and her brothers and sisters had been taken from her forever. Now she prayed that one owner would buy them all. That way, no matter how cruel the slave master might be, they would all be together.

But it was rarely the practice for whole families to be sold on the block as a unit. More often, each family member was put on display alone. Clara watched as the auctioneer hollered for one slave at a time to stand on the block.

Soon her own Margaret was called.

"Ladies and gentlemen!" barked the auctioneer. "Do I hear two hundred dollars for this filly?" Men scratched an earlobe, or adjusted their spectacles to signal a bid on Margaret. She stood tall and proud, emotionless, as the bidding began. Clara was pleased that her eldest daughter displayed such quiet dignity.

"Three hundred?" the auctioneer chanted in his singsong voice. Even the flicker of a buyer's eyelid seemed to be a bid. "This girl is sound in body, and has mind enough to make you a housekeeper. Do I hear three-fifty?" Soon the bidding was over, and a stranger Clara had never seen led Margaret off through the crowd. Where was she going? Somewhere nearby, in Kentucky? Or far, far away, maybe back east to Virginia?

The sun beat down. There was not a breath of a breeze. People fanned their faces with booklets, or pieces of paper, whatever they had that might stir up a little air. Who would they call next? Clara wondered.

It was Richard. Buyers were tough on male slaves. They wanted slaves to be as strong and healthy as good mules, so they could work in the hot sun from daybreak to sundown.

Richard stood motionless while a man from the crowd examined him. His shirt was pulled up so his back could be checked for any scars left from the whips of former owners. A lot of scars meant a disobedient slave. Richard's teeth were examined, the muscles in his arms were felt.

Clara cringed when a weasel-eyed Southern man touched her husband. Deep in her bones, she had a bad, bad feeling about that buyer. He looked like one of those masters she'd heard about, who worked slaves to death picking cotton in the fields of the South. Like broken-down wagons, dead slaves would simply be replaced by new ones.

"What am I offered to get started?" called the auctioneer. The bidding began. Ear scratches and raised fingers and nods increased the price quickly. Soon the bidding was up past one thousand dollars.

Clara mopped the sweat off her eyes with her apron. Then she noticed little Eliza Jane, who was fidgeting beside her. She bent down and wiped Eliza's face. The child was only ten, and she was still suffering from nausea and crying fits over the drowning of her twin sister. When Clara looked back up, her Richard had been sold. So had young Richard Jr. The Southern man had bought both of them.

Eliza Jane was led to the auction block, all clean and fresh in the pink pinafore Clara had laundered for her. But her eyes were wild with fear. She was on the verge of a hysterical outburst. Lord, Clara prayed, bear her up. Give your little girl strength.

But it was too late. Eliza Jane's nerves had churned up her stomach. She couldn't stand still. Suddenly her little body shook violently, and she threw up all over her pinafore. Clara made her way up to the block. The auctioneer tried to stop her, but changed his mind when he saw she had pulled a kerchief from her pocket and was going to clean the girl up. A tidy slave meant more money for him. He let Clara pass.

Clara wiped Eliza Jane as best she could. She gave her daughter a stern look. She'd told Eliza many times that God wanted His children to be obedient. This was God's will. Whatever the reason He had for allowing this to happen, human beings were not to question it. With one look, Clara reminded Eliza of those words. Then she slowly walked back to her place in the crowd.

The ten-year-old was bid on, sold, and led through the crowd. Clara remembered later that it was as if, for the moment, she'd lost her sight. Perhaps she covered her eyes with her hands. Perhaps everything simply went dark. She could not bear to look at her daughter's face. She could not watch as her little girl was loaded onto a wagon with other purchases: cattle feed, a butter churn, and bolts of fabric.

She could only listen as the vendors shouted, the auctioneer chanted, and the locusts buzzed in the still summer trees. She heard the strumming of a banjo, a festive summer song. She heard the wagon lurch forward, and the horses' hooves clip-clop away, taking her little girl farther and farther into the distance.

CHAPTER 4

Freedom!

That day in the summer of 1836, Clara was purchased by George Brown, a man she had never met, but who lived in the area and belonged to Ambrose Smith's Masonic Lodge. In shock after the loss of her husband and her children, Clara remembered nothing of standing up on the auction block, of the bidding, of being carried off in the wagon. She did not even remember arriving at the Browns' rambling white house there in Russellville.

The darkness that flooded Clara that day had seeped into the marrow of her bones. How did such terrible pain go away? And if it did begin to lift, where would it go? For Clara, it was God who absorbed the pain. As she knelt down and prayed, the darkness slowly began to wash away. Clara began to heal.

Little by little, she turned her focus to her life at the Browns'. She was surprised to find that the household was refined and sophisticated, with a piano and a huge library. It was a whole different world from farm life. As a man who made hats for a living, George Brown was a member of the merchant class, wealthier than most farmers. He ran a shop in downtown Russellville and had sixteen slaves to help him pin and sew the fancy hats he sold—hats of silk and velvet, wool and fur.

In the big house, guests were coming and going, going and coming, all the time. The men visitors wore gold watches in their vest pockets, and hats with soft satin bands. They dressed in "Marseilles" cotton shirts—the kind, Clara knew, you boiled with bluing so they would stay white. The women visitors wore the latest hat fashions—silk bonnets with velvet bows and special touches pinned on, like a handful of cherries, or a nest of baby birds. At the Smiths', Clara had worn plain cotton dresses with ordinary aprons. Here, she was given a stylish black uniform with a starched white apron, and a white cap.

The Browns loved Clara, and soon began calling her "Auntie." She enjoyed working in their house, laundering fine lace tablecloths and serving fancy food at their long dining table. They used fashionable china, and six—sometimes eight—pieces of intricately patterned silverware at each place. They didn't eat their meals all at once, but took the time to be served in courses, sometimes seven little meals in one! Clara was amazed that it could take the Browns and their guests all evening just to eat.

But as much as she grew to love living with the Browns, not a day passed that Clara did not think about her lost family. If only her mammy could be here working by her side in this elegant home! If only Eliza Jane could be here, so Clara could teach her the skills she'd learned from her own mammy!

There were times when Clara felt guilty that she had ended up in such a pleasant place, probably better than Richard and her children had. George Brown was kind. He knew Clara's heart was aching. When she asked him to find news about her family, he did.

He couldn't find the men. But he discovered that Eliza Jane and Margaret were both in Kentucky. 'Liza was with the James Covington family somewhere in Logan County, and Margaret with the Bednigo Sheltons in Morgantown. Clara wasn't far from either daughter, but it was too far to be permitted to visit, and letters were out of the question. Although Clara had learned the fundamentals of reading and writing, none of her family was literate enough to read or write letters.

As the years in Russellville moved peacefully from winter to spring, summer to fall, Clara kept the Brown household tidy and well fed. Clara never heard any news, ever, about Richard Sr. and Jr., and her heart finally told her they had been worked to death. But it raised her spirits to know her daughters were both alive and well. For years, George Brown reported that they were with the same owners and seemed to be getting on well. Then one day, he was grieved to tell Clara that

Margaret, still in her teen years, had died of a chest ailment.

Although the news was terrible, at least Clara knew what had happened to her elder daughter. With Eliza Jane, Clara wasn't so lucky. In 1852, George Brown lost track of Eliza. Clara begged him to find out what had become of her daughter. Had she been sold? Although he made inquiries, Master Brown couldn't discover what had happened to Eliza Jane. Four years later, George Brown died.

When his will was read, Clara was shocked to hear that he had left her three hundred dollars! Clara had never had money in her whole life. What would she do with such a huge sum?

She nearly fell over when a second surprise came. Brown's three daughters—Mary Prue, Lucinda, and Evaline—wanted to give Clara the gift of freedom. Freedom? Having money was a strange enough concept. But having freedom? The thought was terrifying and exhilarating at the same time. Fifty-six-year-old Clara had not been free since the day she was born.

Unlike Clara, there were slaves who had to be free. Most slaves, especially those in the Deep South, were treated not only with little respect but often with brutality. Their tortured lives made them long for freedom, fight for freedom, run away every time they got the chance. Over the years, Clara had heard stories of the price they'd paid: lashings, bloody long wounds down their backs. And hangings.

Even Clara had not totally escaped abuse from her

masters. She admitted later in life that she'd been beaten "sometimes," although not often. As well loved as Clara was, and as kind as the Smiths and Browns were, the fact was that all slaves were property. Masters purchased them, owned them, and paid taxes on them to the government. They saw it as their duty to train their property, just as they would train their expensive horses. If a slave got out of line, sassed back, or did anything the master found objectionable, the slave was beaten. Clara, like many slaves, did not make the same mistake twice. She hated beatings, but had never considered running away. Slavery was her life. Right or wrong, she knew no other.

But Clara always knew her soul was free. She could drop to her knees on the kitchen floor, on a hay bale, on a sack of

Drawn from an eyewitness account, this illustration shows the brutal whipping of a Virginia slave named Matt. Torture for disobedience was common, and masters often forced slaves to beat other slaves.

corn, anytime she pleased, spilling out her problems, her joys, her pains. And she knew without a doubt that God listened.

Now Clara felt that God had given her the gift of freedom. No matter how terrifying this uncharted path might feel to her, she would joyfully face whatever the future had in store. She was grateful it was coming easily. She didn't have to fight for it, like so many of those before her and around her.

The Brown daughters had a problem, however. There were Kentucky laws to tangle with. In order to be manumitted—given legal freedom—Clara would have to be put back up for auction. If the Browns bid the highest price, and Clara paid one-quarter of that price, only then could they free her. If anyone outbid them, Clara would end up remaining a slave, owned by someone new.

So, once again, Clara Brown found herself standing on the auction block. The last time she'd been there, she had lost everything she loved. This time, she hoped to gain her freedom.

The auctioneer began his routine. "How much do I hear for this obedient old slave?" The Brown daughters believed that Clara's value on the auction block would be about one hundred dollars. They made their first bid. Immediately, someone bid higher. The bidding continued. Up and up the price went, far beyond their hundred-dollar estimate. Mary Prue, the eldest Brown daughter, kept on bidding, and the price kept rising.

Clara stayed calm. She was certain the Browns would

not let another owner outbid them. When Mary Prue finally bid $475, only silence followed. The bidding was over. The Browns had won the bid! Clara would pay $118.75 for her legal share.

Aunt Clara, at the age of fifty-six, was a free woman!

CHAPTER 5

Up and Down the River

Clara stood outside a warehouse stacked high with sweet-smelling tobacco, grown and dried in the Kentucky sun. The tobacco would soon be loaded onto a flatboat, the same flatboat that Clara herself would be boarding. She would float down the Ohio River until it joined the Mississippi. It was the spring of 1857, and Mrs. Clara Brown was headed for St. Louis, Missouri.

Yes, Clara Brown was now her name. As a free woman, Clara had decided, as many slaves did, to take the name of her former master. After the auction, she worked as paid help for the Brown sisters, saving money. She knew she'd need it. But she couldn't stay long. The laws of Kentucky required manumitted slaves to leave the state within one year. If she stayed longer, she would automatically become a slave again.

At first, Clara had no idea where to go. She did, however, have a clear sense of purpose. She had decided to do whatever was necessary to find Eliza Jane. She wanted them to live as a family again. But where, Clara wondered, should she begin her search?

Just as people had moved to Kentucky and Tennessee in the early 1800s, they were now moving even farther west— to the river towns along the Mississippi and the Missouri. Clara decided it made sense to go with the population flow. Wherever white people went, their slaves and servants went with them.

The Brown daughters wanted to ease Clara's passage to freedom. So they wrote letters trying to help her find work in the river towns. A friend of a friend of George Brown knew of a family in St. Louis. These people, a German gentleman and his wife, were in need of a housekeeper and cook. The Browns wrote a letter of introduction praising Clara as a skilled cook and housekeeper, and a woman of "sterling" character. Clara would take the letter to St. Louis. She hoped that this new family would find her to be the perfect person for the job.

How exciting to be stepping aboard a flatboat and cruising down the river to a whole new life! The boat was basically a large raft with a cabin, where Clara and the other passengers would sleep. Cargo was piled high on board: smoked meats, tobacco, corn, livestock, furs, and leather. Clara clung tightly to the bundle she carried. Everything she owned was wrapped up inside: her clothes, her freedom papers, her letter, and all the money she'd managed to save over the last year.

Her journey began on the Green River. Once a weedy waterway, it had been cleared for transporting settlers, cattle, and produce to river towns downstream. It was a scenic trip. Clara cruised past waterfalls, weepy green willows, and mysterious caves. But it was slow going. The boat had to navigate through the Green River's many locks and dams. Once they reached the Ohio River, travel became easier.

Still, there were dangers. River pirates and Indians often attacked flatboats to steal cargo. For protection, the crew was armed, and three-foot-high planks ran around the sides of each boat. Inside the boarded railing, the journey was lively, with passengers from all walks of life. Somebody always pulled out

An undated woodcut of pioneers in a flatboat on the Ohio River. Flatboats were built without keels, for traveling on shallow rivers. Men steered the boats with one long oar notched on the cabin roof.

a fiddle to play, and people joined in, singing and dancing the evenings away.

During her weeks aboard the boat, Clara's jubilation was often mixed with fear. After a lifetime of answering to owners who controlled her, now she was suddenly making decisions for herself. For instance, how would she go about her search for Eliza Jane? She didn't even know whether Eliza had a last name.

If 'Liza had been sold again, or had run away, she surely would not have chosen the name Covington. She might even have married! That would certainly complicate things. What were the odds of finding a person with only a first name? Or with a last name you couldn't guess if your life depended on it?

Clara worried about her travel decisions, too. Would she find the German family's house when she arrived in St. Louis? She had directions, but she had difficulty reading them. She'd have to rely on strangers for help.

Clara's flatboat reached the "Big River," the Mississippi, and landed at the docks in Cairo, Illinois. There, many boats were continuing downriver to New Orleans, where there was a festival being planned for the very first time. It was called Mardi Gras. Clara, however, would now be traveling the opposite direction—north, to St. Louis.

She transferred to a keelboat, which hardworking boat hands skillfully navigated upstream against the current. When Clara landed at the bustling St. Louis dock, she unfolded her letter and asked a boat hand for directions. Step by step, with her bandanna wrapped around her hair and her precious bundle

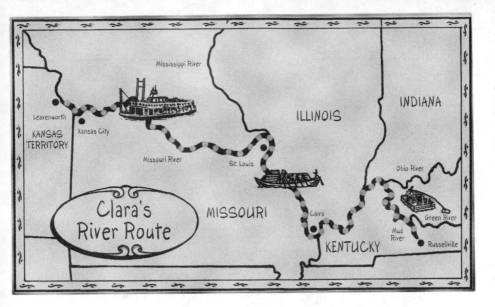

Clara's River Route

Mississippi River · Leavenworth · KANSAS TERRITORY · Kansas City · Missouri River · St. Louis · ILLINOIS · INDIANA · Ohio River · MISSOURI · Cairo · Green River · Mud River · KENTUCKY · Russellville

tucked under her arm, Clara made her way through the noisy St. Louis streets. What a huge city! Over 150,000 people lived there.

Before long, Clara arrived at what she thought was the right house. It was! The Browns' friends hired her as a live-in housekeeper and cook. But before she could start, Clara needed a work license. She was taken to the county courthouse, where the clerk checked and registered her freedom papers and issued her a license that permitted her to work in Missouri.

Because they were from Germany, Clara's new "family" taught her to prepare their favorite foods: sauerbraten and Wiener schnitzel and spaetzle. She, of course, got paid for her work, and had one day off every week. A whole day off!

It wasn't hard for Clara to decide how to spend that time. Not only would she scour the streets and wharves for a sign of Eliza Jane, but she'd let other people know so they could keep on the lookout, too. Every day off, she walked down to the river docks, checking out incoming boats: flatboats, keelboats, and steam-powered paddleboats. Lots of passengers were getting off, and many were loading their goods onto wagons to head farther west.

Never timid, Clara made her way around the cargo and the passengers and the dockworkers, approaching anybody and everybody who looked as if they might help. She asked strangers if they had seen a young woman by the name of Eliza Jane. Clara would then describe her. She'd be about thirty years old—tall, with high cheekbones, and her daddy's big smile. Over and over, Clara held her breath, waiting, hoping.

Her heart leapt every time she thought she caught a glimpse of her daughter. Was that Eliza waving from that packet boat? Was that Eliza, joking with friends beneath that willow tree? Was that Eliza, loading that wagon? Unfortunately, it wasn't Eliza, no matter how many hours Clara spent at the dock; no matter how many times she asked.

As outgoing as Clara was, being alone in a new city wasn't easy. At the Smiths' and the Browns', she had shared quarters with other servants. Everyone had worked together, celebrated together, and cried together. Now she was working for people she barely knew, in a city of strangers.

Clara decided the best way to meet friends with similar interests was to join a church group. She went to a service at the nearby German Methodist church. Escorted to the gallery in the rear for "colored" folks, just like the one in Logan County, Clara found herself warmly welcomed there.

She was invited to meetings where some of the Negroes gathered by themselves, without white folks around to hear their conversations. In private, they spoke openly about news that affected people of their race—especially slavery, and freedom from slavery. In these meetings, Clara began to hear talk of "free" states, where slavery was outlawed and all people were free, no matter what color their skin was. Clara had never heard of such a thing.

The fact was, the laws in the North were clear: no one was allowed to own slaves north of the Mason-Dixon Line, which was the boundary between the Southern "slave" states and the Northern "free" states. Missouri was a "slave" state. It had been ever since the Missouri Compromise had been passed in the U.S. Congress in 1821.

Many Missouri slave owners refused to accept the notion of manumitted Negroes. They hated the thought of Negroes—any Negroes—living freely among whites. These slave owners had blatantly disobeyed the law for many years now, traveling in groups and kidnapping innocent Negroes right off the streets of St. Louis and other towns.

These outlaws were called "nigger nappers." If questioned by authorities, the nappers claimed the Negro they'd captured was a runaway slave with no freedom papers, and that they were the owners. In reality, they were capturing

Negroes they didn't even know, throwing them in wagons, and hauling them back to their plantations to enslave them.

The Mississippi River docks, always busy with travelers coming and going, were a primary target for "nigger nappers." Clara's new friends were worried about her. They felt she was in danger when she wandered down to the dock alone in search of Eliza. For all she'd been through, Clara was still trusting and a bit naive. Just as she and her mother hadn't been afraid of Indians on the Wilderness Road crossing, Clara was not overly frightened about slave nappers. With God watching over her, Clara did not believe she could come to real harm.

Her friends felt differently. The only way to keep from being kidnapped, they warned her, was to have her freedom papers lawfully registered at the courthouse. Then, even if the ruffians tore up her papers, she had legal proof of manumission. They were relieved when Clara told them she'd officially registered her papers when she'd gone to the courthouse for a work license.

It wasn't only Negroes who were concerned about slave nappers. At work, while serving dinner, Clara overheard many intense discussions about increasing violence. Anti-slavery gangs had formed to fight off the growing number of pro-slavery rebels. Fights were breaking out—bloody battles—and they were escalating by the week.

Then, early in autumn, there was alarming news of a different kind. Financial disaster struck the nation. Troubled

CAUTION!!

COLORED PEOPLE

OF BOSTON, ONE & ALL,

You are hereby respectfully **CAUTIONED** and advised, to avoid conversing with the

Watchmen and Police Officers of Boston,

For since the recent **ORDER OF THE MAYOR & ALDERMEN**, they are empowered to act as

KIDNAPPERS
AND
Slave Catchers,

And they have already been actually employed in **KIDNAPPING, CATCHING, AND KEEPING SLAVES.** Therefore, if you value your **LIBERTY**, and the *Welfare of the Fugitives* among you, *Shun* them in every possible manner, as so many *HOUNDS* on the track of the most unfortunate of your race.

Keep a Sharp Look Out for KIDNAPPERS, and have TOP EYE open.

APRIL 24, 1851.

Slave-napping was a problem not only in Kansas and Missouri, but across the nation, as illustrated by this 1851 Boston, Massachusetts, poster.

banks in the East had been anxiously awaiting an important shipment of California gold. Unfortunately, the ship was blasted by a hurricane before it arrived, and all the gold ended up on the bottom of the ocean. Sudden and unexpected, the loss triggered a financial depression that overtook the whole United States. Called the "Panic of 1857," it knocked the prairie states to their knees. Banks collapsed. Railroad construction stopped. People lost their jobs. Many went bankrupt.

Between the financial panic and the increasing local bloodshed over slavery, Clara's employers grew restless. They decided to move west from St. Louis to the more prosperous Missouri River town of Leavenworth, Kansas. As the Browns and the Smiths had done before them, they considered Aunt Clara to be a family member, so they asked her to move with them.

Leavenworth, Clara learned, was a new town, just three years old and full of pioneer spirit. It was a jumping-off point for brave folks heading to California, New Mexico, Oregon, and Utah by wagon train. If Eliza Jane's owners were adventurers, they could very well be thinking of heading to Leavenworth. After nearly a year in St. Louis, Clara had seen no trace of her daughter, and had not received one clue as to where she might find her.

With Missouri getting more and more hostile toward Negroes, Clara thought perhaps Kansas would be more welcoming. Kansas lay directly west of Missouri and, although it was not yet a state, it was a "free" territory that extended way out west to the Rocky Mountains.

To Clara, the move seemed to be a sensible choice. She happily agreed to go.

Dred Scott Case

While Clara lived in St. Louis, she certainly heard about the Dred Scott court case. Scott was a slave who lived in Missouri. His owners had resided for a time in Illinois, a free state located north of the Mason-Dixon Line. Unlike Clara, Dred Scott had not been legally manumitted. However, because he had recently lived in a free state, he believed he should be considered a free man.

His case went before a Missouri court, where judges decided that Scott was right. According to the Missouri Compromise, Scott had become a free man when he'd been taken to Illinois.

Unfortunately, the case was appealed, all the way to the U.S. Supreme Court. In 1857 the court, heavily Southern and pro-slavery, decided that the Missouri Compromise was no longer constitutional because it conflicted with more recent federal laws. The judges decreed that Dred Scott had automatically become a slave again the minute he set foot in the state of Missouri.

The Ship That Sank the Banks

In September of 1857, the SS Central America left California, carrying a million dollars' worth of commercial gold to the East. Secretly, some eastern bankers had arranged for an extra stash of gold to be hidden on board as well—fifteen tons of ingots worth over nine million dollars! The banks desperately needed that gold. First of all, since banks did not then deal in paper money, silver and gold were the only currency they used. Second, the banks were in big trouble because they had loaned out too much money to businesses that were failing. The bankers were holding their breath, awaiting this rich shipment to keep them from going under.

The ship made it through the Panama Canal, but two hundred miles off the coast of South Carolina, a hurricane blasted through, sinking the vessel and all the gold with it. When the news got out, people panicked. They rushed into banks, demanding to take out their money. The banks were broke, and locked their doors. The Panic of 1857 had begun.

CHAPTER 6

Bleeding Kansas

The first thing Clara noticed about Leavenworth was that the whole town smelled like horses. No wonder. High above the river was Fort Leavenworth, the western headquarters for the Army Department, whose main job was to protect settlers from the Indians. The cavalry at the fort branded their tired horses "IC," which meant that, for vigorous military use, they'd been "Inspected and Condemned." They sold at ten or fifteen dollars each, so just about everybody could afford to own one. There were more horses in Leavenworth than Clara had ever seen back in Kentucky.

With the horses came horseflies, swarms of pesky biters that met Clara's boat as it pulled up along the levee. There was a steep bluff covered with hazel brush on the Kansas side, and across the river lay Missouri. Right along the levee was the city, a noisy boomtown with wooden planks covering its muddy walkways.

In 1858, Leavenworth was a community of unsettled people. It felt to Clara as if everybody was on their way to someplace else. The huge stagecoach and covered-wagon company of Russell, Majors and Waddell, a freighting firm, had just built its headquarters downtown the year before. They provided transportation for pioneers heading out to California and Oregon.

Mixed in with pioneers hitting the trail were recently freed Negroes, Missouri slave nappers, U.S. soldiers, and hundreds of families from Germany, Ireland, and Holland. People called the downtown area "Lick Skillet" because the population was as diverse as the ingredients in a stew. Clara settled with her employers in the northern part of Leavenworth, called "Goosetown." Her neighbors were German, mostly, and many raised geese in their yards.

By now, Clara knew the best way for her to make friends was to join a church. She discovered the First Missionary Baptist church, a Negro congregation in Lick Skillet. At this church, she wasn't sectioned off in the balcony! Everyone was equal: they could sit where they wanted, talk when they wanted, and sing as loudly as they wanted.

There, Clara met the first woman who had settled in Leavenworth—Becky Johnson. When Leavenworth became a town in 1854, a local census listed the population as ninety-nine men, and one Negro woman "who took in washing." That washerwoman was Becky. Like Clara, she was a freed slave from Kentucky. Clara and Becky became fast friends.

Just as at the St. Louis congregation, Becky and fellow churchgoers invited Clara to informal meetings. Around the glow of woodstoves and fireplaces in each other's homes, they shared their past stories of slavery, and their new stories of freedom. They helped each other out with food or work or money. They talked hopefully about liberation for all slaves.

Quietly, they recounted how slaves were escaping from the South. Hundreds of runaways were fleeing to freedom through the "Underground Railroad." It wasn't a real railroad, and it wasn't underground, either. It was a whole system of people who believed that slavery was immoral. Acting like railway conductors, they helped fugitive slaves, who were the "passengers," get from the South to the North, station by hidden station.

Clara heard stories that sent goosebumps racing up and down her arms. Runaway slaves hid in caves along the bank on the Missouri side of the river. Huddled in the darkness, they waited for nightfall, when sympathetic Kansans came to rescue them. They followed the conductors into boats and were rowed in the pitch dark across the Missouri River to the Kansas side.

Some of these slaves were from farms in Missouri. Others had come all the way from states like Alabama, Georgia, and Mississippi. These slaves snuck from their plantations by night, followed the North Star across frosty fields, dove deep into haylofts to hide, and slept beneath church pews. They would bury themselves under sacks of potatoes and onions on northbound wagons and hide behind loose boards in old barns, all the time guided by strangers with red kerchiefs tied on their necks—the secret sign of a "railroad" conductor. The slaves ran on bleeding, torn feet; they ran until they reached the caves and crossed the Missouri River to freedom.

Unfortunately, Kansas didn't offer the freedom these slaves were hoping for. The legalities of the Missouri Compromise and the newly passed Kansas-Nebraska Act were difficult for anyone, particularly illiterate slaves, to understand. By now, Clara knew the basic truth: Kansas Territory would not be wholly and legally "free" until it became a state. Congress was planning to grant statehood soon, perhaps within the year. Then the Kansans would vote, deciding the slavery issue for themselves. Most Kansans, Clara knew, planned to vote for a free state.

Their neighbors across the river felt differently. Around 1854, pro-slavery Missouri renegades had begun a campaign to turn Kansas into a slave state. Gangs of armed and violent rebels galloped on horseback across the border, trying to bully Kansans into voting in favor of slavery when the time came. They roughed people up, burned down anti-slavery churches, and shot and killed ex-slaves and those whom they called "nigger lovers." They forced their way into polling places to vote illegally in state elections so that pro-slavery advocates

Border Ruffians invade Kansas. The Border Ruffian struggles over slavery foreshadowed the Civil War.

would gain powerful positions. Wild and lawless, they were called "Border Ruffians."

A rival organization of Kansans, the "Red-Legs," quickly formed to fight off the intruders. Red-Legs and Border Ruffians hid in the hazel-brush patches around Leavenworth, waiting to take potshots at each other. Out in the country, there was open warfare, and many renegades were killed. For Clara, exploding gunfire soon became a daily occurrence. There was so much animosity and bloodshed that, before long, the territory had a new nickname: "Bleeding Kansas."

Clara's employers felt the fear and tension of Bleeding Kansas. Before a year had passed, they decided to move even farther west, all the way to California. Naturally, they invited Clara. As determined as she was to keep moving until she found her Eliza Jane, Clara thought that California seemed too far away, at the western edge of the U.S. territory. The problem was, with her employers leaving, how would she make a living in Leavenworth?

Clara talked over her decision with Becky Johnson. The two friends came up with a great solution. Becky had too many laundry customers. Clara knew all about washing and hanging and pressing clothes. Why didn't Clara start her own laundry business?

Clara got to work right away, even before her employers moved. They gave her permission to use the stove, tubs, and kettle in their home. In the meantime, Becky taught Clara the how-to's of being an independent businesswoman—how to run her own laundry, take in money, and stash away savings. Before long, Clara had saved enough to buy her own laundry equipment.

Over the next few months, life in Leavenworth was tough. The financial depression had made money tight and slowed down everyone's business, including Clara's. And tuberculosis, a contagious lung disease, was running rampant—people could catch it just by breathing infected air. Then there were also rumors of a dangerous civil war brewing. Gunfire between the North and South was not only occurring in Kansas—violence was escalating in many parts of the nation.

Just then, at the lowest point, in late summer of 1858, incredible news came. Gold had been discovered in the "new West," just across the Great Plains—not in far-off California, but in Kansas Territory, in the Rocky Mountains!

"GOLD! GOLD! GOLD!" newspaper headlines announced. It was suddenly the buzz on every street corner, in every church, at Clara's laundry. Could it be true? This was not the first time that folks had heard the cry of gold. Back in 1820, gold was so plentiful in the Rockies, rumor had it, that the Arapaho Indians used solid-gold bullets. The truth was, the Arapaho didn't even have guns. In 1849, there had been the famous Gold Rush in California. That time, although some people lost their shirts, many people got rich overnight. Who knew if this talk of gold could be trusted?

Human nature being what it is, everyone wanted to believe it. All around Clara, hardworking folks had lost their jobs and declared bankruptcy. Their children were hungry, their neighbors were sick with tuberculosis, and their country was on the brink of civil war. Were they ready to hear about instant riches? Were they ready to move to a place with clean air and sunshine, gold-flecked waterfalls, and snowcapped mountains?

For most of Clara's customers, neighbors, and friends, their only question was: How fast can I get there?

The North Star Is My Friend

The "Underground Railroad" got its name in Kentucky, where a slave master had sent hunters and bloodhounds to track down an escaped slave. Slaves, particularly males, were considered a valuable investment of money and time. The trackers searched high and low, with no success. How could the slave have vanished without a trace? In disgust, the master declared: "He must have escaped through an underground railroad."

Other terms became part of the lingo as well. "Who's your friend?" a conductor would ask. "The North Star is my friend," the slave would answer. That phrase was the ticket to freedom for slaves, and they then "climbed aboard," beginning their life-changing journey on the Underground Railroad.

Free or Not Free?

The Missouri Compromise outlawed slavery in all new states and U.S. territories. When Kansas and Nebraska became territories thirty-one years later,

Missourians complained. If they moved to Kansas, they had no intention of leaving their slaves behind. Besides, with Kansas right across the border, it made it too easy for their slaves to run to freedom.

The Kansas-Nebraska Act of 1854 changed former laws, including the Missouri Compromise. It let the settlers of new states themselves determine whether their state would outlaw slavery or allow it, by casting votes. By law, Kansas was a free territory. However, in 1855, Border Ruffians crossed into Kansas, forced their way into polling places, and cast votes. A pro-slavery legislature was elected.

This illegally elected group passed a brutal slave code to protect slavery in Kansas. The Leavenworth Times *explained the code: "Any man who was caught with a newspaper, pamphlet or book antagonistic to the institution of slavery could, upon conviction, be sent to the penitentiary for not less than two years." In his message to Congress on February 2, 1858, President James Buchanan said: "Kansas is, at this moment, as much of a slave state as South Carolina or Georgia."*

CHAPTER 7

"If We Don't Have It, You Don't Need It"

By April of 1859, everyone in Leavenworth seemed to have caught gold fever. All around Clara, the buzz was about Gold Country: the Rocky Mountains, Pikes Peak, the South Platte River, Western Kansas Territory, Cherry Creek, the Gold Fields. These were all terms for the same place, a land out west strewn with gold and prosperity—a place that is now the state of Colorado.

The craziness had begun in the summer of 1858. A band of fourteen pioneers had been panning for gold in Rocky Mountain streams for over a year. Their leader was William Green Russell, a cantankerous Georgia miner who wore his long beard in braids that he tucked into his pants.

These first gold-seekers were a wild and fearless bunch. Like tumbleweeds, they went wherever the winds of prosperity blew them. When they found a spot that looked favorable, they set up big canvas tents and got right to work, panning for gold. Cherry Creek was dry and cracked from the summer heat, but that didn't stop them. For weeks, they crawled along every stream that ran down from the mountains and every dry bed in the foothills.

During the first week of July, Russell and his men hit "pay dirt." They found a handful of gold right where Cherry Creek met the South Platte River. Their find was small but significant. It meant there was more gold somewhere up in the mountains, a cache lode.

Immediately, Russell sent one of his men galloping east to show off his discovery. The rider, Fall Leaf, a Cheyenne scout, arrived in Kansas City on August 26, 1858, displaying the gold.

That autumn, headlines screamed the sensational news. Rumors spread like wildfire. The stories grew grander with each telling. If you dipped your bucket into Cherry Creek, reports said, it would come out overflowing with gold. *The Weekly Times* of Omaha interviewed A. O. McGrew, a grizzly-haired huckster who had pushed a wheelbarrow across the plains. He claimed to have arrived at Pikes Peak with only ten cents in his pocket. But when he'd rolled his wheelbarrow into Cherry Creek, McGrew swore, the wheel came out completely gold-dipped! That did it. Soon Omaha, St. Louis, and Leavenworth were dizzy with gold fever.

So were Clara's customers. Since Clara was the talkative type and a great listener, too, they talked both her ears off.

Had she heard the news? Was it true they had a chance to escape their money woes? Could they, like "Wheelbarrow" McGrew and William Green Russell, strike it rich out west?

Hundreds of men kissed their families good-bye and headed out as fast as they could, before winter set in. Other more cautious sorts decided to take time to prepare. It would take months just to plan, organize, and pack to leave in April or May, when the weather made it safe to cross the plains.

There were so many preparations to be made! They would need wagons and oxen to travel hundreds of miles across the Great American Desert. They'd need axes and shovels to dig for all the gold that was waiting for them. Overnight, Leavenworth changed to accommodate their needs.

Outfitting shops sprouted up like toadstools. "If we don't have it, you don't need it!" boasted the shops. Pamphlets were written with lightning speed and cranked off the presses. "Go West!" they urged. Most of the pamphlet writers had never even set foot out west. They were making plenty of money staying put in the East, producing pamphlets and trail guides that encouraged everybody else to go.

Men hummed songs like "Sweet Betsy from Pike" while they sharpened axes and greased wagon wheels. Women packed preserves and pickled meat, dreaming of gold-roofed mansions. Children sorted through their toys and clothes, giving away what they couldn't carry.

Over the winter, thousands of farmers and bankrupt

The cover of an 1859 pioneer handbook. This and other pamphlets like it described the different routes, camps, clothes, and tools needed for argonauts to trek across the Great American Desert.

business merchants came to Leavenworth and other river towns to outfit themselves for spring, when they would join a train of wagons. Some spent all the money they had in the world on lodging, supplies, and equipment, believing they would make their fortunes out west.

Gold fever was contagious. Little by little, even practical, levelheaded Aunt Clara found herself catching the bug. But her hopes had nothing to do with nuggets of gold. The treasure she was seeking was far more valuable.

Had it really been twenty years since she'd seen Eliza Jane? Her loyal laundry customers kept their eyes and ears open. Still, nobody had ever seen or heard any clue about Clara's daughter.

Was it possible that some gold-seekers were bringing

their slaves out west with them? Maybe the master who owned Eliza Jane—whoever he was and wherever he lived—had gold fever, too?

Clara decided to head west and see. But how would she get there? She knew from her Cumberland Gap trek that the journey would be dangerous. Everybody was teaming up with long wagon trains to stay safe and share supplies. The average cost for three yoke of oxen, a wagon and tools, flour, bacon, and supplies was six hundred dollars, with four folks to a wagon. Clara did not have that kind of money. Could she possibly work her way on a wagon train that was scheduled to make the crossing?

The levee was where outfitters picked up supplies to stock their shops. It was there that wagon masters transferred goods from the boats onto covered wagons bound for Gold Country. One particular April day, Clara took a deep breath and summoned up her courage. She'd cooked up a plan, and when Clara set her mind on something, she was unstoppable. On this day, she was bent on going to the levee to negotiate a deal.

She wound her way past the fish barrels, the mining equipment, and the crates full of tools. Wagon masters mingled with hopeful gold-seekers. They advertised themselves, offering the best prices and the best protection to lead groups across the prairie. Even con artists, who had never blazed trails in their lives, talked like experienced bosses who knew how to handle the dangers of the trails. They gave themselves titles like "Colonel" or "Captain," even if they'd never served in the military. The gold-seekers had a special name, too. Like the intrepid sailors who, in Greek legend, voyaged with Jason in his search for the Golden Fleece, they called themselves "Argonauts."

Clara had sharp ears and good instincts. She could fade into the background and hear things that others didn't listen for. Beneath the bravado of a man's words, Clara sensed intuitively whether he was fair or unfair, sincere or cunning.

She approached a group of men who were talking to a trail boss. If she would do all the cooking and washing, she asked them, would they give her and her laundry equipment passage on one of their wagons?

The men turned, fixing their eyes on Clara. They told her they had no intention of letting some aging slave latch onto their wagon train. Clara raised up her chin and pulled out her freedom papers. She was a free woman, she told them, and a fine laundress and cook to boot.

The trail boss, Colonel Wadsworth, stepped in and took a look at Clara's papers. Clara didn't care how the other men treated her. She wanted respect and a fair deal from the boss. She sensed that Wadsworth had good judgment, a trait essential to the success of the trip. She was right. Powerfully built, Wadsworth was not only a natural leader, but he knew the Western terrain like the back of his hand.

Wadsworth nodded, handing back Clara's papers. So far, it looked as if there would be about sixty people in his party: five families and twenty-six single men. The bachelors, mostly trail hands, could use a good cook and laundress. Could Clara be ready to go in one week?

Clara hurried to find Becky. Together, they jumped for joy, hollered, and celebrated. Clara was going to Gold Country!

Becky teased that Clara was off to "see the elephant." Would she lose everything and come straggling back, miserable and "busted"? Or would she soon be a rich woman, lounging around in one of those gleaming gold mansions in the mountains? Since there were hundreds of miners who needed a clean shirt now and then, Becky figured they'd be paying Clara plenty to handle that chore.

For Clara, the thought of being rich was pleasant, but the gold she really cared about wasn't in the heart of a mountain. It was in the heart of her Eliza Jane. Even though 'Liza would be thirty-three now, Clara pictured her in the sad pink pinafore, her legs trembling, trying to support her terrified body. How she must need a good, long rocking in her mammy's arms! Maybe it would happen soon, in a settlement across the Great Plains, beside Cherry Creek, at the foot of the Rocky Mountains.

Pikes Peak

During the Colorado Gold Rush, Pikes Peak became synonymous with the Rocky Mountains—even though the gold diggings were actually farther north.

The Pikes Peak label was slapped on everything: guns, boots, shovels, hats. There were brand-new outfitting stores with names like "Pikes Peak Outfitters." You could even dine in the Pikes Peak Lunch Room. "Pikes Peak or Bust" became a popular slogan. Many argonauts did go "bust," but others settled in Gold Country and never looked back.

Seeing the Elephant

The story goes that there was a farmer who had never set foot outside his hometown. He dreamed of leaving his hardworking life behind and traveling to far-off, exotic places. One day, a circus came to town. It featured an elephant! Excited, the farmer loaded up his wagon with vegetables to sell, dressed up in his best Sunday clothes, and set off to see the elephant.

When he got to town, he turned a corner and found himself face to face with the biggest critter he'd ever laid eyes on—a real, live elephant! His horses panicked. They bucked and reared and galloped off, catapulting the farmer, his produce, and the cart into a thorny patch of bramble bushes. The farmer struggled to his feet. He was bruised and bleeding, and his clothes were torn to shreds. He'd lost everything: his horses, his wagon, his vegetables, and his Sunday clothes.

"It's okay," he told the shocked onlookers as he brushed himself off. "At least I got to see the elephant."

Pioneer life was full of struggle and disappointment: serious illness, accidents, starvation, bankruptcy, Indian attacks, buffalo stampedes—all threatened the gold-seekers. Even so, the argonauts persevered; because, if they made it, the payoff was worth all the risk.

When a pioneer "saw the elephant," he sacrificed everything in the hope that something wonderful would happen, but often ended up disappointed. Places on the trails were named the Elephant's Backbone, the Elephant's Trunk, or the Elephant Corral. When they passed abandoned wagons or graves, argonauts would say, knowingly: "Well, at least they got to see the elephant!"

CHAPTER 8

The Wagon-Train Plan

The Rig

Colonel Wadsworth planned to take his group by covered wagons, also called "prairie schooners." These were simply sturdy farm carts with canvas stretched on top, over upside-down U-shaped staves. The canvas was contoured to be wind-resistant, able to survive the treacherous gusts of the open plains. Inside, settlers could travel safely: each wagon was a moving home for the women and children, a fort if Indians attacked, a hospital for anyone who got sick, and a dry storage cabinet for supplies. Wagons were slow and cumbersome, making the crossing an eight-week trip. Wadsworth bought fifteen wagons to carry four passengers each.

Animals

For fresh milk on the way, Wadsworth purchased a few cows. To pull the wagons, he bought and branded ninety head of oxen. With two oxen per yoke, that made three yoke (or six oxen) for each wagon. "Bull-headed" was the term coined for these stubborn animals, and they needed lead rings stuck through their sensitive noses to keep them in line.

Hired Help

Wadsworth needed drivers, scouts, bullwhackers to care for the animals, traders, and a cook. He had a cook—Clara, of course—who would also do laundry. He himself was experienced in trading with Indians, and knew what to bring for that. As for the rest, he needed men who were young, strong, and healthy, and who would obey orders. The argonauts, Wadsworth decided, would drive the wagons in the middle of the train. He chose experienced, armed drivers for the front and rear wagons. He hired a couple of bullwhackers, armed men who fed, led, and cared for the animals. They'd walk alongside the train, cracking rawhide whips with twenty-foot lashes to keep the oxen moving. They'd also serve as scouts, and were handy at snapping the heads off rattlesnakes.

Gear

Each wagon was equipped with an axe, a spade, a mallet, nuts, bolts, some replacement hardware, buckskins, a tar bucket, and any other tools needed to handle a breakdown. Every staff member took bedding for sleeping outside: two blankets, one comforter, one pillow, and a canvas cloth to keep it all dry. Clara's cooking supplies included: big kettles for soups and stews, wrought-iron pans for baking bread, coffee pots, tin plates and cups, utensils for cooking and eating, and matches in bottles with tight tops to keep them dry. Each argonaut needed a comb, a brush, two toothbrushes, soap, a belt knife and small whetstone, and a small buckskin bag containing thread, needles, beeswax, buttons, pins, and a thimble. If they wanted, they could bring musical instruments. Harmonicas were best, because they packed easily.

The Route

During the California Gold Rush of 1849, the most popular route to the north was the Oregon Trail, and to the south, the Santa Fe Trail. The routes to Cherry Creek lay in between. Sometimes called "Smoky Hell," the Smoky Hill Trail was the shortest and most direct route to Gold Country. It stretched 680 miles, straight as the crow flies, across the middle of Kansas Territory. It followed the Kansas or "Kaw" River and continued west along the Smoky Hill River branch. At one point this trail left the river and divided into several rough paths. This stretch lasted about fifty miles, but felt like well over a hundred, because it was desert-dry and grueling. It

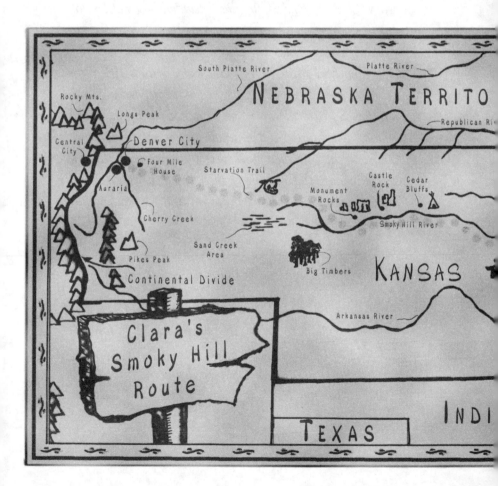

was so perilous it was nicknamed the "Starvation Trail."

Dangers

The Starvation Trail presented the most hazardous challenge for Clara's caravan on the adventure ahead. Many argonauts on previous trips had died of thirst there. If it didn't rain, and the creeks in between dried up, there was no water until the wagons reached the south fork of the Republican River. Wadsworth believed that he knew the fastest desert path and could avoid running out of water.

Another challenge was time. There were no roadhouses along the way to replenish supplies. The argonauts absolutely could not take more than two months for the trip, or they'd run out of food and medicine, and end up as buzzard meat.

A final threat was Indians. In some areas, the Smoky Hill followed hunting trails of the Kiowa.

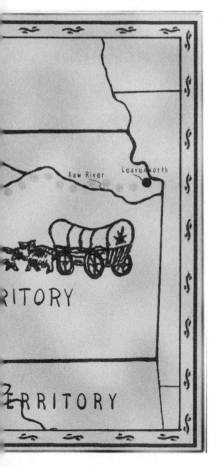

They were fiercely angry about the invasion of so many pioneers, and had lately attacked plenty of passing wagons.

Food

The families carried their own provisions. But what about the twenty-six single men who needed three meals a day for eight weeks? The main meats would be thick slabs of bacon and salt pork, packed in hundred-pound sacks, stowed in salt on the bottom of the wagons so they kept for weeks. The men would hunt if they wanted such fresh meat as birds, rabbit, or buffalo.

Colonel Wadsworth also loaded other supplies: sacks of flour and sugar, stowed in rubber so they wouldn't get wet; saleratus, which served as yeast; as many ten-gallon water kegs as could fit; pickles, dried vegetable slices, dried fruits (mostly apples, for treats); eggs stowed in a barrel of corn meal; vinegar, coffee, rice, and tea. Clara would pick wild onions, dandelion leaves, mint, and other greens on the way. Medicines included quinine, herbs, and some opium. Extra grain—bales of hay—was packed for the oxen, in case the pioneers camped where there was no fresh grass.

Clothing

They would be traveling through snow, rain, sleet, icy cold, and sweltering hot desert. There was the possibility of tornadoes. Passengers packed their warmest, most comfortable clothes. Each man packed flannel shirts, woolen and cotton underwear, two pairs of stout shoes, a rain poncho, and a broad-brimmed felt hat. The women packed plain dresses with high necklines, long sleeves, and dark colors to hide the dirt. They rigged homemade spectacles from flat pieces of colored glass and wire to protect their eyes from the glaring sun.

Rules of the Road

A few days before they planned to head out, Wadsworth called a meeting to brief his passengers. He had them all sign a contract agreeing to look out for each other, to be a team. Pioneers were to take only the household items and personal belongings they needed. Each wagon could carry a total of two or three tons. The lighter the load, the faster the company would move.

CHAPTER 9

Westward Ho!

With oxen snorting, bullwhackers' whips cracking, and families hugging good-byes, off they went. The argonauts rolled out from the Leavenworth landing in mid-April and headed west to find their fortunes. The clear Kansas air crackled with excitement.

Overpacked wagons and inexperienced travelers made for a chaotic send-off. Although Clara's train got off to a solid start, others' didn't. Oxen hooked up by amateurs got loose and "cycloned through the streets," as one argonaut wrote in his diary about that April day. Clumsy wagons overturned and had to be unloaded and repacked.

Some people walked, with all their earthly belongings tied in a bundle on a stick. Others let their mules lug the supplies. There were argonauts on horseback, argonauts in rickety wagons, and argonauts like Clara who were organized in long trains. This trail was no wilderness. A wide, beaten-down path, it was a busy thoroughfare, with faster wagon trains pulling past slower ones, and open-air "privies" on the side of the road, swarming with flies. The road itself was as bumpy as a washboard.

Clara's caravan headed southwest for ten days, toward the Kaw River. Then they planned to travel due west all the way to the Rocky Mountains. That first day, as far as Clara could see, the prairie was wide and wild, with dots of white yarrow and purple thistle swaying in the ocean of buffalo grasses. There were no twisting climbs, no treacherous rivers for the oxen to cross, no narrow mountain passes like those on the Cumberland Trail. Instead they passed rolling hills, little towns, and clear springs. They found plenty of wood to pick up along the way for the nightly campfire.

Clara and most of the other argonauts walked beside the wagons. They stopped at noon, and Clara cooked supper, the main meal. Memories of her mother on the Wilderness Trail must have surfaced as she rolled up her sleeves and got to work. The men helped her haul out the big kettles and set up the lugpole to hang them over the fire. They started the fire in a pit left over from pioneers who had preceded them.

For cooking, Clara was on her own. Even as a slave, she had never prepared a meal so fast for so many people. There was coffee to boil, meat and vegetables to brown for the stew, and pan bread to bake. Afterward, there was a mess of plates and forks and spoons and cups and pots and pans to clean up and stow before the train rejoined the big parade. At dusk, when they camped for the night, it was time for Clara to cook another meal, a lighter one, mostly using leftovers from the "nooner." Soup or chili sufficed.

That night, as the men sat around the fire, Clara sized up their glowing, bearded faces. These were the men who would be in her care the next eight weeks. Some were gentle, with genuine smiles and grateful winks for the grub. Others were rowdy young adventurers, probably away from home for the first time. A few looked just plain mean. They were as venomous as rattlers and proud and loud about being Missourians.

Colonel Wadsworth took time to remind the company of some procedural matters. First, the men would take turns on night guard, watching out for Indians who might steal the cattle. Second, the women would sleep in the wagons, while the men slept on the ground.

A nasty discussion followed. Should Clara be allowed to sleep in a wagon? Absolutely not, the Missourians proclaimed. She wasn't white, so she should sleep with the cattle. Besides, she was hired help, and all the women passengers had paid an extra fee for the luxury of sleeping inside the wagons.

That first night, and most nights, Clara slept wrapped in blankets beneath a wagon. Like the men, she laid a canvas down first, to repel water and dew, then tucked herself in under a comforter. Clara may have slept inside on stormy or frigid nights, when the weather was too cruel to make her stay outside.

On the second day, Clara got into the flow of a regular routine that would last for the entire trip. Every morning, in the freezing dark before dawn, she crawled out of her blankets and got to work. While the other women each prepared meals for their own families, Clara cooked for her twenty-six men.

Breakfast preparation started with coffee. Clara roasted whole green coffee beans over the fire until they turned brown, milled them through an iron grinder, cracked a fresh egg into the grounds, and set the pots over the fire. For the biscuits, she stirred in fresh milk from the cow. She soon had bacon sizzling, eggs frying, biscuits baking, and coffee boiling. Breakfast ready, Clara banged a spoon on a tin pan to wake up the men. The minute they finished eating, she washed the stacks of dishes in a pot of creek water she'd boiled and stowed them in the wagon.

By first light, it was time to hit the trail. The young argonauts were eager to get the ox teams hitched up and moving. They wanted to cover six or seven miles by noon. Any slowpokes could catch up later.

By midday, the men had worked up ravenous appetites. The team slowed to a halt near a stream for their daily "nooner." The oxen were unhitched for a drink and a nap. It was time for Clara to make the stew for supper. She swatted flies from the meat, checked the stream water for mud, and searched the grasses to find fresh herbs to toss in the pot. The men could sprinkle a bit of gunpowder onto their own helpings if the stew wasn't salty enough for them.

Before Clara could take a breath, the "nooner" was over. The men repaired any faulty equipment and hitched the oxen back up to the wagons. The team scrambled to rejoin the raggedy parade, and rattled and clattered along the crowded, bumpy trail about five more miles, until the sky showed the first flaming orange streaks of sunset.

When they found a grassy enough place to camp, the drivers swung the wagons around in a circle and corralled the animals inside. Now Clara prepared a "lick skillet" of beans or soup with leftover bread. Dessert was dried fruit, or an occasional apple or wild-berry cobbler, sprinkled with sugar.

Clara came to look forward to the evenings. One by one, the stars came out. Argonauts were camped all around. The campfires of nearly a hundred cozy settlements lit up the prairie.

Still, it wasn't time for Clara to rest. She settled into quieter chores, the kind of work she'd done on the Smith farm. She milked the cows, letting the warm milk sit in a pail overnight. In the morning, she'd skim the cream off into a wooden bucket and hang it inside a wagon. The bumpy ride would churn it into butter. She bandaged the blisters on her feet and mended holes in her shoes and socks, which were already wearing thin from the rocky trail.

Meanwhile, parents took time to school their children and, settling on the riverbank or boulders, some pioneers wrote in their

An illustration of Clara on the trail, by Hendon Davis, from a 1949 article in *Colorado Magazine* celebrating her journey.

daily journals. Families sang and danced. Men played harmonicas and fiddles and told stories around the campfire.

Many nights, particularly after a few swigs of "tanglefoot" whisky, the men got into bitter arguments about the most heated issue of the day—slavery, and the possibility of the Southern states seceding from the Union. At times like these, Clara wisely faded into the background and settled down to sleep beneath a wagon. The prairie sounds were a lullaby of chirping crickets, whooshing winds, and crackling firewood. Her muscles aching from the long day, perhaps Clara prayed for stamina to make it through this grueling trip. Certainly, she prayed that she would find Eliza Jane somewhere at the end of the trail.

Sundays were a day of rest. Clara's team stayed in camp, not only because the Christian travelers demanded it, but also because it was a break for the oxen. If there was a preacher with any of the neighboring caravans, he would conduct prayers. But most of the time, the argonauts held services of their own, praying and reading from the Bible. The open prairie and the wide blue sky was their church.

After prayers, the men would fish, hunt, and mend wagons and boots. Clara did laundry, sewed shirts, hung meats to dry into jerky, and nursed wounds. She made bread that would last for the whole week. If she could squeeze it in, Clara took some time to nap amid the steady lull of the prairie winds.

After three weeks on the trail, one day seemed much like the rest. Then, suddenly, in mid-May, the landscape changed. No longer green and fertile, this was dry grassland, flat as a platter. When a hill covered with trees appeared far ahead, it was so unusual that the argonauts knew exactly what it was. They'd been warned in the small settlements along the way that Cedar Bluffs was a hideout for Indians.

Sure enough, that day, the first sign of danger came. Scouts sighted a long dark line off in the distance, moving like a shadow across the grasslands. Panic set in as the news shot from wagon to wagon. Those were Indians—columns and columns of Kiowa! Men grabbed their guns, and women closed the flaps on the canvas, clutching their children tightly inside the wagons. They prepared for the worst.

Slowly but surely, the Kiowa approached, until Clara could hear their beads clinking. They rode silently, the chiefs leading, warriors and squaws with papooses behind them, and bony dogs yapping at the horses' hooves. Clara, walking tall beside the oxen, did not share the terror of her companions. After all, her mother's Cherokee blood flowed in her veins.

"It's the white folks who were to blame in them Indian troubles," Clara declared later in her life. As on her Cumberland Gap journey fifty years before, Clara's heart went out to the Indians. This was their land, the land of the Delaware, Potawatomi, Pawnee, Comanche, Cheyenne, Kiowa, and Arapaho. For centuries, they had been the only people here, hunting antelope and buffalo in the winter. Clara understood how alarmed they must be by the sudden invasion of wagon trains.

Hours passed as the convoy rolled on, trailed by the shadow of the Kiowa. Finally, a chief gestured to Wadsworth. The colonel answered him, not in spoken language, but with hand signs and facial expressions. Clara and her team watched as Wadsworth and the chiefs sat down in a circle for a parlay, a friendly chat, and passed a peace pipe to smoke.

Wadsworth offered them tobacco, sugar, and alcohol. In exchange, he wanted moccasins for his men, who might soon be crossing mud and snow. The bartering done, the Kiowa split away from the wagon train. All that the Indians had wanted were provisions! The argonauts were greatly relieved.

New sights and experiences helped make the endless stretch of the Great Plains tolerable. Soon they saw a peculiar rock formation that jutted straight up out of the flat landscape like a spired castle. Wadsworth knew that Castle Rock marked the midway point in their trip. Then, just two days later, there were more giant rocks. Called Monument Rocks, they were made of chalk and rose sixty feet high, almost a gateway to the West. The land from then on went back to being flat.

For the first time in her life, Clara saw prairie-dog towns, miles of mounds that they passed through and camped beside. The argonauts were constantly entertained by the busy critters, who must have been as astonished as the Indians to see the pioneers. Antelope were new, too. Slim and graceful, they loped across the tall, dry grasses. Screaming black-and-white magpies darted for rodents.

As days turned into weeks, and weeks into a month, the pioneers' initial excitement began to wear thin. They were becoming trail-weary, and the unpredictable weather did not make it any easier. "Blackbird storms," cold and unexpected, thundered across the skies and dumped torrents of rain at night, leaving the morning trails a mess of muddy ruts. It was a chore for Clara just to keep the sugar, flour, and scraps of firewood dry. Some days were so scorching hot that the wood shrank. The wagon wheels had to be removed at night and soaked in the river to keep their iron rims from rolling right off during the day.

One morning the argonauts awoke, their faces white with frost, their bedding frozen to the ground. A blizzard was rolling in. Quickly, Wadsworth had the men dump barrels of provisions out of the wagons so there would be room for everyone inside. They pulled out the extra hay they'd packed to feed the oxen, in case of just such an emergency. Huddled in the wagons, surviving on crackers and jerky, the argonauts spent two days trying to keep out the blasts of icy wind.

Even when the weather was pleasant, there were challenges. Wagons were always breaking down. If they couldn't be fixed, they were left in a heap by the side of the road. Food, tools, furniture, clocks, and family heirlooms were abandoned when they got to be too heavy to carry. So many piles of books were thrown away that people called the stacks "prairie libraries."

The bumping and jolting of the wagons made some women and children queasy, so they walked. That left room inside for any men who were fighting off colds or pneumonia. Clara began nursing the sick with medicinal roots and grasses she found growing on the prairie. Plants she knew from Kentucky grew here, too. She could use yarrow compresses to stop severe bleeding, and comfrey to heal cuts and scrapes. She boiled chamomile and thistle into tea that settled upset stomachs. As sturdy as ever, Clara herself didn't get sick, even though she continued to walk every single day.

By now Clara recognized tracks left by jackrabbits, prairie mice, deer, and antelope. Soon new tracks showed up on the trails—large hoofprints. They were traces of buffalo. Clara began to see buffalo wallows, the deep depressions left from the animals rolling in dust to coat their fur and cool themselves off.

She and the other women and children began collecting buffalo chips as they walked. The dried, grassy, pancake-flat droppings were used for fuel. Early in the trip there had been wood to gather for burning, but now there were no trees at all, not even along the river. Luckily for Clara and the other cooks, the chips smelled like sweet hickory wood as they burned.

Soon they were near Big Timbers, another astonishingly tall, dense cluster of trees that looked like a distant cloud of smoke. There was a sudden rumbling in the ground under Clara's feet. Then a small dark shape appeared against the horizon. It barely seemed to be moving. The shape grew longer and wider. It was far too massive to be a band of Indians. The sound, like a distant drum, swelled until Clara was afraid its vibration might make the ground cave in.

"Stampede!" bellowed the bullwhackers. Wadsworth immediately corralled his team into a circle. Soon, an entire herd of buffalo came into view, pounding nearer. Three or four hundred of the monstrous, shaggy-headed animals thundered toward the argonauts. The pioneers shot off rifles. Dust clouds billowed, stinging Clara's eyes and nose. Luckily, the herd veered away from the shots and bypassed the wagons.

When the dust settled, Clara had a new talent to add to her list. She could still darn a sock and pluck a chicken and cure a sick patient with herbs. She could mend a shirt or a shoe and knew how to cook and clean and launder. Now, besides all that, Clara Brown could roast a whole buffalo and use the leftovers to whip up a tasty stew.

Mountain-Man Lingo

Buffalo cider—*Fluid from the stomach of a buffalo, drunk by mountain men and Indians to quench thirst*

Bull cheese—*Jerky made from buffalo meat*

Calaboose—*Jail*

Crimpy—*Frigid cold, as in "a crimpy day"*

Furry bank note; also, a "plew"—*Beaver pelt (worth good money in trade)*

Grease and beans—*Grub, or food*

Gully washer—*A torrential rain*

Hair of the bear—*A high compliment from one*

mountain man to another (for example, "He has the
hair of the bear")

Leeverite—Any abandoned item on the side of the trail,
as in "leave 'er right here"

Pay dirt—Earth with enough precious metal in it to be
worth mining

Yunk—Youngster

Trail Grub

Campfire—Every day, Clara would search for enough
dry wood or buffalo chips for a long-lasting fire. The
men would straddle the stew pot across a "lugpole,"
then lift it to rest like a spit over the fire on standing
support logs. They had to use moist green wood so it
didn't burn.

Muddy water—When streams were muddy, the water
was undrinkable. Clara put cornmeal in a jar with the
water to strain out the mud. Eventually, the mud
would sink to the bottom with the cornmeal, leaving
the somewhat cleaner, usable water on top.

Prairie chairs—It was nice for argonauts to have a
comfy chair to sit on as they ate their grub. As
provisions were used, the empty barrels were made
into chairs. The men cut out one side, stuffed the
barrel with hay to make a seat, and used the curved
shape as a back to lean against. And what happened with

the extra planks they'd cut out? They used them for firewood, of course.

Sourdough—*Clara made her own yeast by stirring flour, salt, and sugar into boiling water. After a few days in a covered jar, it would sour, and serve as a yeast starter for her loaves of bread. Each day, Clara added a bit of dough back in so the starter could last the entire trip.*

CHAPTER 10

The Starvation Trail

The *Rocky Mountain News* later called it the "route for the foolhardy and insane." Prairie dogs scurried in and out of their mounds, barking what seemed to be warnings at passing wagons. Skeletal remains of earlier journeys lay along both sides of the trail: ruined wagons, discarded stoves, and the bones of dead oxen. The Gold Rush created a bellyful for the buzzards. They hovered, searching not only for animal carcasses, but human carcasses as well.

It was about May 24, and Clara's wagon train was now trekking across the part of the trail that gave it the nickname "Smoky Hell"—the sandy, dusty stretch between the head of the Smoky Hill River and the south branch of the Republican River. The temperature was 90 degrees, and Clara's shawl was all she had to shade her head from the glaring sun. The grasses, drained of their spring green, had burned to yellow-brown. There wasn't a tree in sight.

It turned out that Wadsworth's route was no easier than the others across this stretch. The middle trail he'd chosen was shorter by over a hundred miles, and that was the advantage. One extra day on this part of the trail could make the difference between survival and death. Under Wadsworth's leadership, this team would not lose their way, and could hope to stay on schedule.

As expected, the small creeks had dried up and groundwater was too deep to dig for. As was dreaded, not a drop of rain fell. The oxen lumbered along at a snail's pace, barely able to cover five or six miles each day. Water, the one thing that people and animals could not live without, was tightly rationed.

When they'd left Leavenworth, Clara's convoy had packed all the water kegs they could fit on board. They had refilled them all before leaving the Smoky Hill River. But no matter how much they carried, it wasn't enough. The argonauts were thirsty, and the oxen were thirsty. The cows were too parched to give milk. Clara tried thirst-killing tricks the experienced argonauts showed her, like sucking on a stone, a bullet, or better yet, a piece of dried apple.

Dragging her feet across the rocky trail, Clara felt this was like hell, being that the hell she'd learned about was scorchingly hot, cruel, and waterless. Her teeth and tongue and ears and eyelids were coated with sand, as were those of everyone else. Tempers flared, and arguments started. Often the arguments led to fistfights, which could escalate into gunfights. Wadsworth tightened his command; he threatened troublemakers with expulsion if they could not act decently. Some members of Clara's convoy ended up going off with other groups.

About two weeks before, Clara's group had begun meeting up with teams coming back the other way. They looked even more pitiful than Clara's company. Many were staggering along on foot, because their oxen had given out. At least Clara's team still had a spark of hope in their bloodshot eyes. These "go-backs" looked beaten. Why were they traveling east?

They poured out their disappointed hearts at night around the campfires. In 1858, these pioneers had headed to Cherry Creek with adventurous spirits and high hopes. They'd "seen the elephant," all right.

There was no gold, they told Wadsworth's party. Not one nugget had been found in over a year. The only people who were prospering in the Rockies were a slew of shady politicians who had carried their wealth with them from the East. The whole Gold Rush was a hoax, a humbug created by promoters and newspapers and guide publishers, all based on the tiny handful of gold that Fall Leaf had carried to Kansas City the past summer. The only people getting rich were the folks who sold the gold pans, equipment, clothes, supplies, guidebooks, mules, and oxen. They hadn't gotten rich from mines, but from *miners.*

Those who had stirred up the gold excitement in the first

place were now knee-deep in trouble. Disappointed gold-seekers were hunting them down. False tombstones were erected along the trails with threatening inscriptions. Referring to two well-known guidebook writers, one was inscribed:

"Hang Byers and D. C. Oakes

For starting this damned Pikes Peak Hoax."

The go-backs also reported more danger ahead. There were land thieves in Cherry Creek, they warned, and robbers on the trail. There were piles of dead snakes, and live ones, too—sometimes two hundred—of all shapes and sizes. There were decaying human bodies. At one spot up ahead, they said, twenty-two people lay dead.

Hearing these stories, hundreds of wagons began turning around, returning to Kansas and Missouri. A few of the wagons in Clara's party joined them. During that spring of 1859, about forty thousand pioneers gave up and went home. It was hard for Clara not to be discouraged.

If Eliza Jane had started off with a group of argonauts, had they turned back, too? It was impossible to know. At this point, it was farther for Clara to go back than to finish the journey. Not a fainthearted woman, she decided to continue on.

It only got worse. Mirages shimmered in the distance, sparking hopes that the Republican Fork lay just ahead. Some days the dust flew so thickly that Clara could barely see the oxen right beside her. Like the rest of her companions, she rubbed axle grease on her split and blistered lips. The heat wrung her dry of every ounce of energy. She forced herself to continue walking, even when her swollen and aching legs wanted to give out beneath her. Oxen dropped. Men fainted.

Clara spent more time nursing than cooking now. There wasn't much left to cook, anyway. Supplies had grown scanty. Even with the best planning, wagons could only carry so much. Six or seven weeks into the journey, meals were meager and had to be made with non-perishable ingredients like flour, salt, and dried fruit. On those days that the men didn't find rabbits or snakes to eat, Clara had to create meals without eggs, milk, butter, vegetables, herbs, or meat. Mostly, she scrounged up flapjacks, crackers, or flatbread, with perhaps a bit of jerky.

There were more graves now. It seemed that Clara saw one every hundred yards or so, with stacked rocks or wooden scraps from a wagon for a headstone. Occasionally the survivors had left remembrances, like a saddle with a bullet hole in it, or the decaying skull of the horse that had died with its rider.

On about the thirtieth of May, when some argonauts recorded in their diaries that they had been without one drop to drink for forty-eight hours, the scouts cried out the word everybody had been waiting for: "Water!" Squinting, Clara made out a thin silver streak far ahead on the horizon—the Republican River! Excitement flashed through the wagons. Spirits soared. The minute the oxen were close enough to smell the water, their heads perked up and their nostrils flared. They went crazy, leaping ahead to get a drink, bumping and jolting the wagons along with them.

The argonauts went half-crazy themselves. They jumped from the wagons, pails and ladles in hand, and raced to the river. Many leapt right in, splashing and swallowing down gulps. Some broke out in tears. Parched, exhausted, and grateful, Clara knelt down by the riverbank in prayerful thanks.

They camped by the Republican Fork for two days. Clara had all the water she needed for laundry and cooking. She could prepare tea again, and make stews and soups with broth whenever the men found meat or fish. After the cows had rested, there was a little fresh milk. The worst was over.

The argonauts hit the trail again on June 1. Within just a few hours, they caught their first glimpse of snowy white peaks. The Rocky Mountains, at last! Clara could see from Pikes Peak all the way north to Longs Peak, with a stretch of lavender Rockies, frosted white, in between. Rugged and grander even than the sweet Blue Ridge Mountains of her childhood, the Rockies didn't emerge out of gradually rolling hills, but jutted suddenly at the end of the flat plain, as if they'd been dropped from the sky.

The closer the wagon train got to the mountains, the more the whole landscape began to change. Now Clara saw wildflowers—scarlet and purple and bright yellow—and cottonwood trees sending fluffy white seeds into the air. And there were chokecherries, the flowering trees that gave Cherry Creek its name. Clara chuckled. Trees? They were scrawny and gnarly brush, compared with the spreading oaks and chestnuts of Kentucky.

As she trudged on, past more graves, past broken wagons, past pioneers returning east, Clara kept her eyes fixed on the snowy Pikes Peak range, the biggest in view. It seemed to take forever to actually get to the mountains. Distances were deceiving in this wide land, and they still had about fifty miles left to travel—four or five long days.

Lying under the huge sky of stars at night, did Clara wonder what lay ahead? Did she wonder what challenges and surprises were in store for her? Wrapped in her blankets, she heard packs of coyotes wailing through the night, at home in the place she herself would soon also call home. Now and then, the howl of a solitary wolf pierced the silence under the waning moon.

In the light of day, when the prairie dogs began squeaking and scurrying in and out of their dusty mounds, Clara heard a clatter of excitement. Up toward the front wagons, scouts were telling Colonel Wadsworth about big news coming from Cherry Creek. More gold had been discovered!

It was the seventh of June, and Clara's company was anxious to hurry ahead. They stopped for the night four miles outside the Cherry Creek settlement, at a small shanty where they could replenish their supplies and camp for the night.

When they arrived, they found a gathering of pioneers in high spirits, celebrating. A prospector named John H. Gregory had recently ridden down from the mountains into the Cherry Creek settlement carrying with him a vial of gold. The first gold seen since the summer of 1858, it was worth a small fortune—eighty dollars! Red-haired, rowdy, and dislikable, Gregory had found what every argonaut dreamed of finding— he'd discovered a whole lode of gold!

By now, Clara knew that a lode was a vein that led to lots more gold. It was much better than placer gold, the kind they panned for in the creeks and rivers. A lode meant there were hunks of gold deep inside the mountain. Men were digging up gold worth sixty, eighty, even one hundred dollars in one day! The argonauts stayed up into the night, energized by the incredible news. The next morning, they hurried as fast as their oxen would tramp.

On Wednesday, the eighth of June, Clara's wagon train came to its snorting, hollering, rumbling stop at the confluence of Cherry Creek and the South Platte River, right between two new towns. Not one, but two settlements had been established at the Cherry Creek Diggings—Denver City and Auraria. There'd been so many "go-backs" that only about three thousand people were in the towns right now, so there was plenty of room for new settlers.

Local townsmen directed Clara's caravan into a

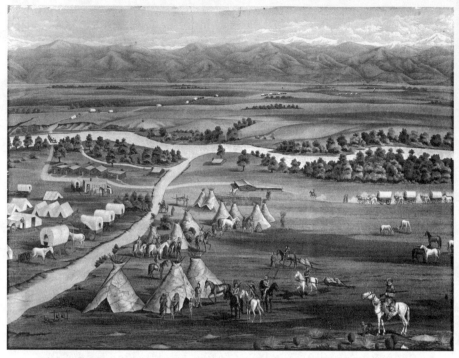

The confluence of the South Platte River and Cherry Creek in 1859. Auraria and Denver City were still wilderness settlements mixed with Arapaho and Cheyenne camps. Denver City lay on the east bank of Cherry Creek and Auraria on the west.

gargantuan cattle yard in the center of Denver City—the Elephant Corral. The wide-eyed pioneers blinked, trying to get a sense of their new home.

What did it look like, being there at last? To the south was a cluster of Arapaho and Cheyenne tepees. Next to them was a slew of canvas pioneer tents and a scattering of half-built cabins, mostly deserted. There were larger tents with such crudely painted signs as "Grocery," "Doctor," "Lawyer," and "Land for Sale." There were certainly no kingly palaces, no churches with shining gold spires. This capital of Gold Country was just a dusty road on a dried-up riverbed, with a few buildings on each side, mostly saloons.

And here was Clara. She fixed her gaze to the west, where the famed snowcapped mountains loomed. Not at all disappointed, and full of high hopes, Clara dropped to her knees, thanking God for seeing her to the end of the trail. She prayed for guidance in her new life and, more than anything, prayed hard for help in finding her Eliza Jane.

How to Treat a Rattlesnake Bite

The Prairie Traveler, *one of the famous 1859 guidebooks, suggested several methods of saving a fellow pioneer who'd been bitten by a venomous snake. One tried-and-true method was to get down and suck out the poison, "repeatedly spitting out the saliva." The next step was to chew on plantain leaves, slap them on the bite, sprinkle tobacco powder on top, and wrap up the whole mess in a rag. Dried turtle blood would work as a fine replacement for the plantain.*

The Prairie Post Office

Many argonauts kept journals on the trail. It was a relaxing pastime, and a way for them to keep a record of their daily adventures. They also enjoyed writing letters. Since there was no established way to mail them, "prairie post offices" were created— wooden barrels set along the trail where pioneers could drop notes inside. They gave advice or warnings or simple encouragement to other travelers. "Watch out for rattlers near the prairie-dog town," they might say. Disreputable argonauts sometimes led others off in the wrong direction, or scribbled notes about preposterous, false, gold discoveries.

Blue Brothers

The three Blue brothers, Daniel, Alexander, and Charles, traveled from Illinois to Gold Country at the same time that Clara did. They took the Smoky Hill Trail and veered off on an unexplored shortcut through the Starvation Trail. Seventy-five miles east of Cherry Creek, they got lost and ran out of food and water. To survive, they resorted to cannibalism.

Daniel Blue made it to Denver City, and on May 12, 1859, he made the following statement: "Alexander, my eldest brother, died, and at his own last request, we used a portion of his body as food on the spot, and with the balance resumed our journey towards the gold regions. We succeeded in but traveling ten miles, when my younger brother, Charles, gave out, and we were obliged to stop. For ten days we subsisted on what remained of our brother's body, when Charles, expired from the same cause as the others. I also consumed the greater portion of his remains, when I was found by an Arapaho Indian, and carried to his lodge, treated with kindness, and a day and a half thereafter brought to Denver City."

CHAPTER 11

Hurry Up and Get Rich!

When Clara's company of argonauts straggled in off the trail, they were a sorry sight: hungry, grimy, and in need of shelter. But before they could set up camp or find a hotel or even get a bite to eat, the local people descended on them like fleas.

They were full of advice: Quick, trade in your oxen, wagons, and trail tools, outfitters advised. In exchange, argonauts could get mules or horses or whatever they needed to get settled. The corral was piled with red-flagged items being auctioned off. Locals swarmed in to bid on old wagon wood for fuel and on tired oxen to butcher for food.

Grab your gear and start mining, prospectors advised. Hordes of argonauts—well over half the newcomers who'd arrived so far in May and June—had moved up to the mountains to hunt for gold near Gregory's Diggings. The argonauts were urged to buy stagecoach tickets, land claims, and mining gear to help them get started prospecting in the hills. Red-flagged shovels, picks, handcarts, and clothing could be had for twenty-five cents.

Promoters from both Auraria and Denver City elbowed their way in, encouraging Clara and her companions to stay and settle in their town. Each was trying to gain a reputation as "the" Cherry Creek settlement. Auraria, founded by Russell and his miners, meant "the place of gold." Its population was bigger than Denver City's, and was growing hour by hour. Denver City, founded by a politician named William Larimer, had more saloons and businesses to boast of. From where she stood, Clara thought the towns looked identical.

All this talk was enough to make her head spin. All Clara wanted was a good meal, and a place to stay until she found accommodations. Most of her wagon team felt the same. As more caravans pulled in and the locals hurried to welcome them, Clara's team said their good-byes and began to scatter off in different directions. Some went to find a good place to pitch a tent for their first few nights. Some headed straight for the Denver House, a popular hotel and saloon attached to the Elephant Corral.

People were rushing around like a bunch of restless prairie dogs, sniffing out the fastest way to get situated, get fed, and get rich. Levelheaded Clara was not about to be dragged into a newcomer's panic. For a few minutes she stood on Larimer Street, getting her bearings and absorbing the scene.

What a motley bunch of folks had come to Gold Country to make their fortunes! There were gamblers and miners, dolled-up ladies and refined shopkeepers. There were genteel men in tailored suits and starched white shirts, called "black-legs." There were tan-faced frontiersmen, "buckskins," who wore faded leather clothes with dangling fringes of glass beads.

Indian children were down by the creek, launching buffalo chips at one another while their mothers looked on. Clara noticed other Indians wandering around wearing flannel shirts and elegant plug hats, along with their deerskins and buffalo-leather vests. There were Mexicans, and lots of "breeds"—folks of mixed ethnicity. There were other Negroes, mostly men, wearing cowboy hats and stitched boots.

Because of her experiences in the river towns and on the trail, Clara had been concerned about how Negroes were being treated in the Cherry Creek towns. Seeing this lick-skillet mix of people, all looking as if they fit right in, she decided she had little to fear. One newly arrived doctor, who set up a practice in town, wrote in his diary that on June 13, there were "quite a number of Negro women, with a pleasant but scanty sprinkling of white ones, and a mixed population of white, black, red and yellow."

At first glance, Clara saw no Negro women, which meant, of course, no sign of Eliza Jane. But she wasn't worried. She had heard that a few Negro women, mostly

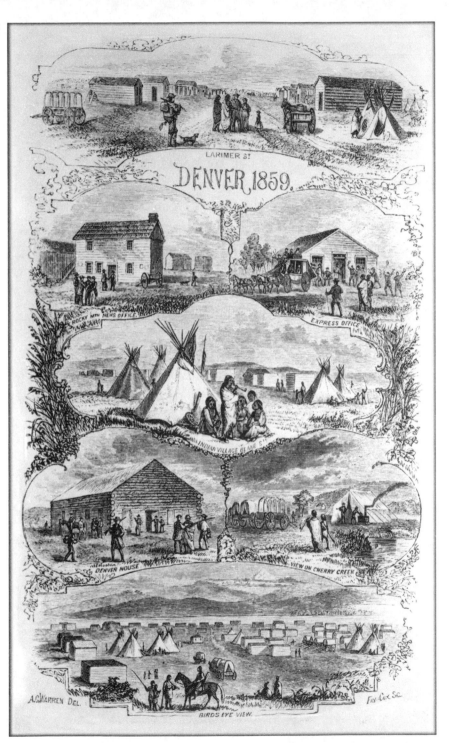

LARIMER ST

DENVER, 1859.

ROCKY MTN. NEWS OFFICE.

EXPRESS OFFICE

INDIAN VILLAGE BLAKE ST.

DENVER HOUSE

VIEW ON CHERRY CREEK

A.C.WARREN DEL.

FRY-COX SC.

BIRDS EYE VIEW.

working as housekeepers, had recently arrived. Besides, she'd just barely rolled into town, and she was patient. She knew everything good would come in its time, including Eliza.

A group of Clara's trail companions invited her to the City Bakery on Ferry Street, across the dry creek bed in Auraria. The restaurant, with a few roughly made tables and a counter, served good home cooking, twenty-four hours a day: fresh bread, apple and mince pies, and cakes. After the last few weeks of flapjacks and trail crackers and muddy water, it was a welcome and cozy spot. The hand-painted sign above the counter read: "The proprietors E. Karczewsky and H. Reitze will accept as payment gold dust, flour, dried apples, etc."

The "H. Reitze" named on the sign turned out to be a young, white-headed German whose name was Henry. Clara and Henry were friends from the start. One interest they shared was church worship, although religion was not a priority in new mining towns, Henry told her—there weren't many churchgoers. But a small Methodist congregation, all men, held services wherever possible. They prayed in tents, in saloons, or under the willows by the creek. Clara was more than welcome to join their next prayer meeting.

Some good news, Henry told Clara, was that several Methodist preachers were on their way out from the plains. They planned to set up two missions: one in Cherry Creek and one up in the mountain mining camps. Two of the men were Jacob Adriance and John Milton Chivington. Adriance, a lean and soft-spoken preacher, would arrive from Omaha any day.

Chivington, who would come later, had been Henry's pastor back in Nebraska. Big as a barn, he stood six feet four inches tall, and was famous for his bellowing hellfire-and-damnation sermons.

Clara made an immediate decision. She would do everything in her power to help establish the Methodist church in Gold Country. She would begin by attending the next prayer meeting. Eventually, maybe she could even hold prayer meetings in her own home.

Now she had a second decision to make. She needed to find work. Clara figured that most work came to newcomers by word of mouth. She let Henry know that she could bake or cook anything, from German-style black-forest cakes with coconut frosting to Southern-style fried chicken with buttermilk biscuits to camp-style beans and buffalo stew. Need be, she could roast a whole ox, she joked. She was also an excellent laundress, and had all her own equipment to get started.

There was competition from other laundries in town, but new customers were bumping in off the trail every day. Very few men out here knew how to cook or launder well, and they were always in search of a woman whose talents reminded them of home. Henry agreed to spread the word, and was certain Clara would have plenty of work once she got settled.

Speaking of settling, Clara needed a roof over her head. Some of her argonaut companions planned to camp. Not Clara.

She'd had enough of the frosty nights and dusty winds and venomous snakes. Was there a place she could rent? she asked Henry. She was delighted to hear that many of those empty cabins had been abandoned by bankrupt miners, and were available not to rent, but to purchase. If she wanted, Clara could buy one for twenty-five dollars!

By nightfall that very first day, Clara Brown moved into her own little one-room house in Auraria. It had a mud roof, a dirt floor, and log walls of gnarly cottonwood. It was no golden mansion, but it was perfect for now. It was big enough to accommodate a laundry business and prayer meetings, and it was sturdy enough to keep out snow and dust, coyotes and bears.

The cabin smelled woodsy, and Clara warmed it up with a good fire in her stove. She tightened the muslin fabric that was stretched over the paneless window openings. She settled in that night on the pile of hay in the corner that served as a bed. After fifty-six nights on the trail, Clara was ready for a good long sleep.

Hot off the Presses

Go-backs had threatened William Byers, a promoter for the city of Omaha, Nebraska, because he'd written several infamous guidebooks to the gold fields. But fiesty, twenty-eight-year-old Byers still had the guts to trek out to Cherry Creek, arriving just two months before Clara. He lugged his thousand-pound printing press all the way across the plains in a wagon with THE ROCKY MOUNTAIN NEWS *printed on the side, advertising his future enterprise.*

Determined to start the town's first newspaper, Byers got to work fresh off the wagon train. Not wanting to alienate either Denver City or Auraria, he set up his shop on thick stilts, smack-dab in the middle of Cherry Creek, between both towns.

A rival publisher had already arrived. He announced that his newspaper would be called the Cherry Creek Pioneer, *and that his first issue would be out in four days. Byers hurriedly set up. He barely had time to hire help, research, write, and print his paper. His team, which included his wife's brothers, a scrawny frontiersman named Scout Wiggins, and a Negro typesetter named Jack Smith, went nonstop. Not sleeping a wink, they worked straight through the four days, and straight through a spring snowstorm that leaked trhough the roof, onto the press and the candles they needed for light. Just before midnight of the fourth day, his first Friday in town, Byers emerged from his temporary "office," triumphantly handing out copies of the first issue of the* Rocky Mountain News, *dated April 23, 1859.*

The Cherry Creek Pioneer *rolled off the presses*

twenty minutes later—exactly twenty minutes too late. Nobody bought it.

A Jumping Town

The Cherry Creek area was jumping, in more ways than one. "Jumping," in western slang, really meant "stealing." An argonaut could stake out a claim for a mine or a piece of land or a home, but it wasn't legal until it was put on paper. Town-jumping, cabin-jumping, and claim-jumping were all common.

The minute the first few cabins were built in 1858, the jumping started, with each new band of frontiersmen taking over the property of some current settlers at gunpoint.

That November, William Larimer had been sent from Leavenworth by Governor Denver of Kansas Territory to stake out a town. Armed, and backed by his men, Larimer jumped the claim across the creek from Auraria. Rumors spread that his men threatened to hang anyone who got in his way. Whatever happened, Larimer made a deal with the claim-owner from Lawrence, Kansas, and called the new town Denver City.

Once he'd gotten what he wanted, Larimer turned into an upstanding citizen, bringing his wife and nine children out to join him, and becoming the first mayor of Denver City. He made sure that nobody else jumped his land the way he'd jumped theirs. So their names would go down in history, he and his associates named the streets for themselves: Larimer, the main steet, followed by Lawrence, Curtis, Blake, Wynkoop, McGaa, and Bassett; and, to keep peace, also used some local Indian names: Arapaho, Champa, Cheyenne, and Wewatta.

CHAPTER 12

Wild and Woolly West

The Game of Life was created by Milton Bradley in 1860, right around the time Clara's life out west began. Called The Checkered Game of Life at the time, it was a game of making money and losing fortunes, of finding jobs, buying insurance, and owning a home. Success or failure was based on a spin of the wheel. So was life in the early Cherry Creek towns.

Everything was a gamble, and that suited these settlers and fortune hunters just fine. There were no banks. People carried six-shooters to protect their money. There was no insurance: people built up houses and businesses, even though fire or flood could wipe them out in a flash.

In the saloons, patrons drank whiskey and played poker twenty-four hours a day, seven days a week. Armed men lounged against log walls, spitting on the dirt floors, and watching as the founders of Cherry Creek used city lots for poker chips to bet on anything and everything, even next winter's first snowfall. There were nights when all the land and buildings in the area belonged to someone else by the time Clara woke up.

During her first balmy June night in Gold Country, Clara barely slept a wink. With no glass windows to close out the noise from the high-spirited, razzle-dazzle town, the sound of whooping and singing and gunshot blasts poured into her cabin. All night long the streets were jumping, and the carousing didn't stop till sunup.

Clara wasn't the only sleepless one. Horace Greeley, editor of the *New York Tribune,* wrote that there were "more brawls, more fights, more pistol shots with criminal intent in this log city of 150 dwellings than in any community of equal number on earth." Greeley had journeyed west to get the real gold-rush story, firsthand, for his readers, and had rolled in just weeks before Clara. He hadn't gotten a full night's sleep since his arrival.

On Thursday, the ninth of June, 1859, Clara woke up to a sound she'd hear every morning from that day on—the rapid patter of an auctioneer. Hearing the booming voice must have made her think of the Logan County slave auctions, but she soon learned it was the red-flagged argonaut items that were being sold, not people.

Clara climbed out of her bed of soft hay, cheerful and determined. She organized her washtubs and baskets. She would need a table for her ironing, wood to burn in her stove, and some customers. Unlike the local gamblers, Clara did not believe in luck. She believed in hard work and steady faith. Wrapping her bandanna around her hair and smoothing out her pinafore, she stepped outside to the breathtaking sight of rosy early light on the mountains.

She went from one argonaut to the next, drumming up laundry business. By the end of her first week she had a few customers, including some sent over by Henry Rcitzc. She laundered everything from fine white shirts for the "black-legs" to clay-caked pants for the prospectors.

It was different doing laundry out west. The summer breeze was so hot and arid that everything dried in half the time Clara was used to. There were no mosquitoes to swat, no gnats buzzing around her ears as in Missouri and Kentucky. Instead, there were wild animals. Occasionally, a lone buffalo would come stampeding through town, sending dust flying. She learned to watch out for the bears, especially the grizzlies that came down from the forests for food. They were still not used to sharing their wilderness home with people.

In this new settlement, every day brought surprises. In Clara's first weeks, right before her eyes, the gritty settlements of Auraria and Denver City turned into towns, each vying to outdo the other. Cottonwood trees were chopped down by the hundreds and cut into logs for building. Carpenters ran out of nails and had emergency shipments sent by wagon train. Nearly every day, Clara would see a building that hadn't been there the day before.

By July, Denver City and Auraria were real, honest-to-goodness boomtowns, with: eight hotels, nine boarding houses, eleven restaurants, twenty-three saloons, four lumberyards, four ten-pin alleys, two theaters, a post office, a newspaper, and many lawyers, doctors, real-estate agents, cabinetmakers, blacksmiths, butchers, carpenters, shoemakers, jewelers, and laundries.

All these businesses were needed because reports said that 150,000 people had set out across the Great Plains and would arrive in Cherry Creek by the end of summer. Although many of those argonauts turned back before completing the journey, there were now five hundred new settlers arriving every week!

On the heels of the boom came the criminal element. The *Rocky Mountain News* reported that crime was expanding by leaps and bounds. The town's master blacksmith, "Noisy" Tom Pollock, had to wear a few new hats: marshal, whipper, hangman, and undertaker. He earned fifty cents a head for each offender he caught. Since there was no jail, he locked them in rooms in his downtown hotel, the Pollock House. As punishment, Pollock publicly whipped gold thieves and card cheaters. A gallows was built to hang worse offenders: murderers and horse thieves.

As the Wild West carried on around her, Clara kept to her mission. Going about her daily business, she began asking about Eliza. She was especially hopeful that the Negroes in town might have some news, since most of them were either

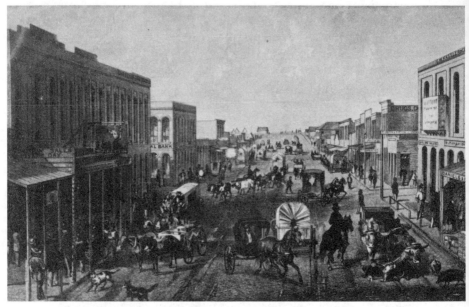

Soon after Clara's arrival, Denver City became a bustling boomtown. This photograph shows Blake Street and The Elephant Corral (center left) in 1861.

runaways or freed slaves whose paths might have crossed Eliza's somewhere along the way.

Among the Negroes and mulattoes Clara met were Jack Smith, pressman for the *Rocky Mountain News*, and Ed Sanderlin, an ex-slave who now ran a barbershop. There was congenial "Uncle" Sims, who owned a restaurant on Larimer Street, and Jim Beckwourth, a famous trapper and scout, who managed the local trading post where Clara sometimes bought soap. None of them could help her make headway in her search.

Clara's laundry customers, who changed continually, couldn't help either. Every single day, argonauts arrived with trail-dusty clothes and gold-crazed eyes, got some sleep and some decent grub and clean clothes, stayed a night or a week or a month, and then headed up the canyon to Gregory's Diggings.

That's where the real gold was. As ornery and disreputable as John Gregory was, his mine had turned out to be a bonanza, and the mountain towns were expanding like mad. It was hard for Clara to find stability, with so many friends and customers constantly moving on.

She was thankful when Jacob Adriance arrived in midsummer! Jacob turned out to be a minister in training, soon to be ordained. Early on, he wrote in his diary: "Moved into a cabin. Had supper all alone, bread and stewed peaches. I feel a little lonesome."

Jacob's meager dinners and loneliness didn't last long. Clara decided to bring over homemade soups or stews, and pies or loaves of bread almost every evening. Jacob was delighted, not only with the food but also with Clara's enthusiasm in wanting to help get the Methodist church off the ground.

He encouraged new argonauts to join in Clara's prayer meetings during the week and attend Sunday services in his cabin. At every service, Clara passed the word about Eliza

Jane, asking people to pray that her search would be successful. Clara was pleased to be part of a growing congregation. Within three months after Jacob's arrival, there were sixty people in the church. Soon, in November, Reverend Chivington showed up and presided over some of the church groups in the foothills and the mountains.

Clara found the perfect way to help the preachers, particularly Jacob. Tattered, hungry argonauts often knocked on his cabin door. Jacob invited them to sleep on his dirt floor, and he turned his old travel trunk into a makeshift dinner table.

Soon Clara was bringing enough stews and pies to feed the minister's whole flock of lost sheep. If a prospector was ailing, Clara could be up to her elbows in soapy water, but she'd take a break to stop by Jacob's cabin with hot soup and motherly advice for herbal remedies.

The seasons came and went, and Clara flowed with them in her new home. In autumn, she pickled and canned and dried whatever fruits and vegetables were available. There were plums and strawberries that grew wild, and some potatoes and onions that came from the brand-new farms started by settlers who'd arrived in time for spring planting. The most abundant fruits were the red chokecherries, so tart that eating them off the vine caused the taster's whole face to pucker.

The local Cheyenne and Arapaho were experts on chokecherries and other native plants. Clara got to know them, and made friends with an Arapaho-Sioux woman named Jennie

Jones. From Jennie, she learned the secret of making a good chokecherry jam: lots and lots of sugar. The Indians had only begun using sugar after a handful of pioneers had visited and stayed to live in the 1840s. Some of the Indians had married white pioneers, including Jennie, who was the wife of a rowdy frontiersman with two different names: William McGaa and Jack Jones.

Many people took on new names out west, Clara discovered. Some did it to hide from the law, but others wanted to create a more professional identity or simply fit in better. Jennie had changed her name to please her husband. She was also planning to send their son to school when the time came.

Going to school was a new concept for most Indians. They had always educated their children at home, in the traditional ways of their tribe. All that began to change when an Irish teacher named Owen J. Goldrick arrived in September and started formal classes in his cabin. He taught reading, writing, arithmetic, astronomy, and chemistry, charging each student three dollars a month.

So many families with children had arrived since summer that soon the school expanded into a larger cabin. Clara helped start a different sort of school herself that November: the Union Sunday School, which met in Jacob's cabin.

For all her good work in Denver, Clara felt restless. The search for Eliza Jane had come to a standstill. If she could earn—and save—more money, she could travel the country looking for Eliza. But with all the laundry competition in town, and with the instability of her customers, how could she make the money she needed?

An early snowfall on September 28 brought prospectors by the hundreds drifting down from the mines, escaping the weather and bragging about their gold. Most intended to winter over in Cherry Creek, and return to the mountains at the first sign of a spring thaw. They complained to Clara how there was not one washerwoman in all of the mountain towns. Men went for months, waiting to return to Cherry Creek to have their clothes cleaned. Was this the answer to her problem? Clara wondered. Perhaps. But she didn't have to make a decision just yet.

Before Clara knew it, it was Christmas Eve, 1859. Swags of pine and holly trimmed windows and doorways. Horses' harnesses were strung with bells, jingling through town, lanterns lighting their way. There was a party for the Sunday school children, and Clara, Jacob, Henry, and other members of the Methodist Church got gifts together for them.

The wealthy "black-legs" celebrated with a lavish private dinner. In an elegant spot just outside of town, William Larimer and his well-to-do friends served up a spread of oysters and buffalo tongue, swan and grizzly bear. Always trying to add to their wealth by promoting Denver City, they sent the menu back east for the newspapers to publish.

The poorer "buckskins" stayed in town, where bright red

bows on the saloons invited guests in to celebrate with all-night poker games. At midnight, townsman Dick Wootten came crashing in from New Mexico, driving a wagonload full of Taos Lightning, a whiskey made of wheat. Moved with holiday spirit, he shared the whole load with homesick miners who had no families to keep them warm. Hundreds of argonauts drank their Christmas cheer right on the streets, in the deep-freeze weather.

To Clara, Christmas meant sharing God's love with close friends and family. Turkeys were plentiful. Clara bought several at two dollars each and made stuffing from a favorite Southern recipe she'd been taught back in Russellville. She and her friends had a merry evening celebrating in Jacob's little cabin in the glow of a corn-stub fire.

That night, Clara listened carefully as Jacob and his new associate, Reverend George Fisher, told their friends about plans for a new church. Denver City and Auraria were arguing about which town deserved a real church building. Frustrated by the rivalry, the two ministers had made a decision. Since the heaviest population was up by the mines, they wanted to build the first church up there.

Clara had already felt a tug toward those snowcapped mountains to the west. Now she was certain God was calling her not just for earthly work, but for spiritual work, too. Her first Christmas in Cherry Creek would be her last for twenty years.

Christmas Lights

There were lots of Christmas trees that year, since settlers only had to walk a few steps up the mountain to cut their own pines. However, there weren't too many candles lighting up the branches. Tallow candles, made of animal fat, cost one dollar each in early Cherry Creek!

There were few beeswax candles, because the first beekeeper in town had just arrived. He had to leave the honey and the wax in the hives for the first year, since the bees needed them, so everyone had to wait until the following summer for local honey and candles. Fish and whale oil were the most common fuel for wick lamps. Settlers were happy when kerosene was discovered in 1859. It burned cleaner, didn't smell bad, and, by 1860, was easy to find in town.

The Money Game

In the early days of Cherry Creek, goods had been traded by bartering. There were no dollar bills then. The U.S. Treasury didn't start printing greenbacks until 1862. By late 1858, the mines were producing, and gold dust became the accepted currency.

Argonauts carried pouches filled with the gold powder, fine and shiny and yellow, and if they wanted to make a purchase, they'd shake a bit of it onto a scale. A merchant weighed it, just like cinnamon, or black pepper, or sugar. Smart buyers had tiny pocket scales of their own, to make sure they didn't get cheated.

A small pinch of gold dust held between the thumb and forefinger was worth about twenty-five cents. It would buy men a shot of whisky, a shave, or a Missouri newspaper, ten days old. It would buy Clara a couple of eggs, a pint of beans, or lots of meat, because deer, antelope, and buffalo were plentiful.

For the unscrupulous, there were infinite ways to steal gold dust. Some saloon-keepers scraped extra dust off the bars, then scratched their beards with sparkly fingertips, waiting until nobody was looking to shake out their earnings. Others scooped dust into their fingernails. There were miners who greased up their hair in the mornings, and when the boss wasn't looking, removed their hats down in the mines. Gold dust collected in their sticky hair. That night, they'd brush out their secret take-home pay.

The First School

Owen J. Goldrick was a scholarly Irishman who dressed in a black silk hat, boiled shirt, and a frock coat with solid gold buttons. He had everyone buzzing when he rolled into town in September. "In his lavender gloves, he held a bullwhip and was urging his ox team on with Latin curses," wrote one reporter.

Goldrick bought a cabin and set up a school within two days. The thirteen students in his first class included children of Indian, Mexican, and white parents.

CHAPTER 13

When the Stars Fell Thick as Tears

Many years before Clara arrived, the Indians who lived at Cherry Creek had been warned by their ancestors to be very careful of intruders. An old Cheyenne wise man named Sweet Medicine had gathered members of his tribe in his lodge before he died.

"Listen to me carefully," Sweet Medicine is said to have told them. "There are . . . people . . . that you will meet someday, toward the sunrise . . . good-looking people, with light hair and white skin. These people do not follow the way of our great-grandfather. . . . They will always try to give you things, but do not take them. . . . They will try to change you from your way of living to theirs," he warned.

The Arapaho, too, had early premonitions. In November of 1832, there had been a dazzling shower of shooting stars in the night skies above the Rocky Mountains. The Arapaho people saw something in those stars that no one from back east had seen—an omen.

"The stars fell as thick as the tears of our women shall fall when you come to drive us away," Chief Bear Hand had told white pioneers. Bear Hand predicted that soon white people would steal all the land and run the Arapaho out of their homes.

The cluster of lodges that Clara had found when she first arrived formed a plain and simple community. There were no saloons, no shops, and no newspaper office. Surrounded by buffalo grasses and wildflowers, the camp was an oasis of quiet for Clara. The men hunted, fished, and defended their tribe. The women stayed in camp, caring for their children, cooking, and preparing buffalo hides: stripping, beading, and stitching them into beautiful clothes.

Even with the warnings from their ancestors, the Arapaho and Cheyenne people did not attack the pioneers when they arrived. Friendly by nature, these tribes welcomed them as guests, trading with them, allowing them to build their strange shelters, and sharing occasional meals.

Curious about their new white neighbors, they visited Denver City and Auraria often. There, they found things they'd never seen before: sugar and soap, guns and nails, prepared foods, perfume, and china. They had begun to trade furs, moccasins, and beaded jewelry for these unusual luxuries.

They did find it strange that many pioneers didn't treat them as equals. Jennie told Clara about her son named Denver, who'd been born in March. Although Little Denver was the very first baby born in town, because he was a "breed," his birth didn't count to the governing townsmen. They waited for an all-white baby to be "officially" named the city's firstborn.

This was just one of many incidents that troubled the Indians about their new neighbors. So was the way the white men scarred the earth. They cut down the cottonwood trees along the riverbank to build cabins and stores. They tore up soil to irrigate, re-routing the sacred river water onto their farms.

The Cherry Creek Indians were willing to live peacefully with their new neighbors. They hoped to come to a mutual understanding about the land that served as their hunting grounds. Over the past few years, too many mis-understandings had led to the murders of both pioneers and Indians.

Eight years before Clara's arrival, in July of 1851, ten thousand riders from local tribes, including the Arapaho and Cheyenne, had gathered at Horse Creek for peace talks with the soldiers at Fort Laramie. Warriors on horseback galloped in with painted faces, chiefs wore ornate feather headdresses, and each brave dressed in dignified tribal finery.

During the parlays, the soldiers took common phrases from the Indians' mouths and incorporated them into their own language. "Great White Father" became the name they used for the president of the United States, making him appear to be a benevolent leader. It was the "Great White

Father" in Washington who had sent gifts—blankets, beads, tobacco, food and drink, even a full-dress general's uniform for each chief.

The soldiers used the word "treaty" as if it solved everybody's problems. Words were important to the Cheyenne and Arapaho. They trusted that, to the white strangers in their fancy blue uniforms with polished gold buttons, words had the same significance.

The treaty they signed at Horse Creek in September of 1851 supposedly insured that the Indians could keep most of the land that is now western Kansas and most of Colorado. Pioneers had the right to travel through these areas, but could not build towns and fences, stake out land, or farm the soil.

The Treaty of Horse Creek was still in effect seven years later, when Russell found gold in Cherry Creek. It was still in effect when towns were staked out. It was still in effect when Clara arrived to a fancy city-in-the-making, with its saloons and its cabins, its post office and newspaper.

Clara could see that, in the few short months since she'd come, the Indians were changing. Their land was being taken over by pioneers; renegade braves were killing argonauts on the trails; and the treaty did not seem to be working as planned. With many buffalo being killed for sport, and native plants being trampled by the towns' expansion, the Indians were losing their food supply.

Many of Clara's Indian friends had begun to rely on the pioneers for food. Jim Beckwourth spent more time in the

Cheyenne village, trading his manufactured goods for Indian treasures. Indians were sometimes breaking into cabins to steal sugar and soap and wheat flour.

Clara noticed that Little Raven, a cordial Arapaho chief who wore metal hoops in his ears and a fine tailored jacket, was socializing in town morning, noon, and night. When the pioneers first came, he had told them he hoped they would not stay too long. Now he spent less and less time with his own people, and far more time in the saloons with the frontiersmen. Had he forgotten the elders' warnings?

"Listen to me carefully," Sweet Medicine had said. "They will keep coming, coming. . . . There will be many of these people. So many that you cannot stand before them."

Life Before the Gold Rush

The Arapaho and Cheyenne tribes had shared the land at the foot of the Rocky Mountains for generations, living with the mountain lions and cinnamon bears and elk. The only human enemy they knew were the Utes, who lived up in the mountains.

No invasion by the Utes, however, could match the sudden invasion of argonauts, whose covered wagons clattered along the hunting trails, kicking up billows of dust, leaving behind a trail of eaten grasses and buffalo carcasses.

The Indians believed the land was a gift from

the Great Spirit, and that human beings should leave it in its natural state. They did not farm. They considered tearing up soil to plant potatoes or carrots to be unnecessary and disruptive of nature. They ate only what they found, like berries and wild roots. When they put up tepees, they tried to disrupt the land as little as possible. They only killed buffalo and antelope if they needed them for food, shelter, and clothing.

CHAPTER 14

Clara's Golden Nest Egg

Christmas had come and gone. So had Clara. She had moved from Auraria up to the mountains, and now it was March 1860. This was where the new Methodist church would be, because this was where the miners were.

And where there were miners, Clara figured, there was money to be made. She hoped to earn enough to travel for the rest of her life, if she had to, to spread the word about her long-lost daughter.

It had been a challenge to find a ride up. Non-whites, even though they could purchase a home, could not travel by stagecoach. It was against the law. So Clara, who plowed through problems like they were bothersome fences, tracked down a fellow argonaut who'd been on her wagon train.

She paid him to join her on the stagecoach trip, nearly forty miles uphill, a steep climb of four thousand feet.

Pretending to be his servant, Clara dressed in her shabbiest calico, wrapping a bandanna on her head, and not a living soul suspected that it was this quiet old "colored" lady who'd paid for passage.

Mountain City, soon to be called Central City, had been a bit of a disappointment at first. After all, it was called "The Richest Square Mile on Earth." Rumor in Denver had it that gold dust was so plentiful, you could scoop up handfuls right off the streets. That wasn't quite the way Clara found it.

One long, muddy road snaked up through town, lined with makeshift wood buildings. A thin coating of brown dust hung heavy in the air, mixed with smoke from blasting powder: Since the heavy deposits of gold lay deep inside the mountains, the miners dynamited huge sections of rock to get into the veins and lodes. The creeks were clogged with mine tailings (residue), and with silt and sludge from the gold-digging. Most miners were living in tents that clung to the mountains, as if ready to topple down when the next good wind blew in.

When Clara arrived, she'd found a two-room cabin on Lawrence Street, with a woodshed attached. In the main room, she had her stove set up for heating her boiler and iron. There was plenty of space in this room for prayer meetings. The second room was just for her. Her log bed was piled with hay, and heavy spikes were nailed to the wall for a closet. The attached shed was stacked with wood for her stove, and there was space on the floor for anyone who might need a place to stay.

The day after she arrived, Clara hung a hand-painted sign outside. It simply said: LAUNDRY. Most of the miners were still down in the warmth of the Cherry Creek towns for the winter. Even so, the minute that Clara's sign went up, customers flocked in. The Gold Rush had created heaps of filthy, mud-caked clothes, and no womenfolk to wash them.

As Central City grew in the 1860s, it became not only the economic center of Colorado Territory but the cultural center as well. The rear of the saloon in this photograph contained a reading room, and the bookstore sold leather-bound volumes of Shakespeare.

Living in Central City was expensive, since all the food and goods had to be shipped in from the plains. A smart businesswoman, Clara decided to raise her prices to meet the cost of living, and she charged fifty cents a shirt. Since Clara ran the only laundry in town, the miners were willing to pay the price. And since the red and blue flannel shirts they wore didn't need boiling or bluing, and didn't take much ironing, it meant she could launder shirts in half the usual time.

Living and working in Central City was a whole new adventure for Clara. The noise from the mines was aggravating. Every day she heard the blasting of dynamite and the constant chinking of picks and axes. The stamp mill hammered repeatedly as it crushed rocks to expose the gold inside. Whenever a mine caved in or there was another emergency, the shrieking whistles sounded their alarms.

At the same time, nature in the mountains was peaceful. There were Stellar's jays, sapphire-blue, that screeched much louder than the jays back in Kentucky. There were eagles and hummingbirds and yellow-bellied marmots and white-tailed deer. The local squirrels had pointy black ears and hopped like bunnies through the snowy pine woods. Not just bears, but mountain lions, too, could surprise Clara when she was outside hanging clothes or getting water.

Spring brought peculiar weather. In April, Clara was ready for tulips and daffodils, and windows flung open for spring cleaning. Instead, the snow outside the wavy panes of her cabin windows came down as solid as a sheet hanging on a line. Just getting to the outhouse was an adventure. Clara had to fight through deep drifts, her hands and face numbed by the time she returned to the cabin. She had to hang blankets on the walls to keep the flakes from blowing in, and to melt pails of snow by the fire to get water. No wonder all but the hard-core miners were still down in the plains!

A young Negro handyman, Henry Poynter, had toughed out the winter in Central City, working for several local families. When Clara found out that Henry lived alone in a tiny cabin, she insisted that he come over for a nice meal. He was the same age her daughter Margaret would have been, had she survived.

Immediately, Clara "adopted" Henry, and soon had him over for supper almost every night. Clara cooked and Henry paid for his share of the food. On clear evenings, Clara and young Henry had an awesome view. They'd watch the sun as it set, painting the clouds with rose and gold and turquoise, like transparent colorful veils.

Henry was just the first of Clara's many adopted family members. Jeremiah Lee and Lorenzo Bowman were two more. Jerry, who'd been in Leavenworth at the same time as Clara, had arrived on a wagon train just two weeks after she had. He'd come up to Central City with Lorenzo, one of the most experienced miners in the area. They were prospecting for gold and silver.

That first snowy spring, Clara fed them her famous soups and stews, often made now with venison, elk, and bear meat. Neighbors caught sight of Clara kneeling on the ground at times where Jerry and Lorenzo were mining below, praying out loud for God to protect their work.

Clara was a beam of light—not just for her adopted family members, but for many people in town. One early morning at about five o'clock, an attorney was trudging unhappily up Eureka Gulch, near Clara's cabin. He began to hear "songs of praise and expressions of joy." Up ahead, he spotted Clara, with a basket of clothes on her head, singing as she strode along. He watched while she sat down to rest, with her load of laundry beside her, and started clapping her hands and shouting, "Bless the Lord! Bless the Lord! I am so happy this morning!" He decided that Clara must have some secret to life that he didn't. He became one of the first members of the local Methodist church.

When buds finally began to sprout on the aspen trees in May and columbine shoots pushed up through the rocky ground, the miners came back from Denver. Yes, they told Clara, it was called Denver now. After all the competitive arguing, Denver City and Auraria had merged, celebrating with a festive moonlit ceremony on the bridge over Cherry Creek in April.

Miners kept coming—by stagecoach, on foot, on horseback, by mule train. More argonauts had crossed the plains this spring, so there were more prospectors than ever. Suddenly, Clara was the only washerwoman in a town of fifteen thousand men!

Life in Central City was like Denver ten times over: ten

times as wild, ten times as woolly. At night, hundreds of campfires dotted the mountainsides. Added to the clatter and rumble and blasting from the mines was the noise from the miners in town. Gunshots rang through the streets day and night. Miners had noses bent crooked from fistfights. Murders and hangings were weekly events.

Although some miners were thriving, most made about ten dollars a week. Clara earned ten dollars for every twenty shirts she took in. That would buy her all the flour, sugar, canned vegetables, meat, tea, soap, and fuel she could possibly use in a month. The rest she could stash away for Eliza Jane, and use to help a few folks in need.

And Clara, who liked people, was a magnet for the needy. She knew how isolated it could feel in the mountains, especially when the snows packed you in for days at a time, and you'd start talking to yourself just to hear a human voice. Some men went all winter without seeing a soul. Worse yet, she heard that they also went without changing their long underwear, so the hair on their legs knitted right into the fabric by spring!

Clara made sure that destitute prospectors had full meals and a place to sleep in her shed until they got back on their feet. In return for her generosity, many optimistic miners promised Clara partial stakes in their future profits, when they finally hit pay dirt. Jerry and Lorenzo insisted that the deals be put on paper, in the form of contracts to protect Clara's interests. Soon Clara, who had forgotten how to write her own

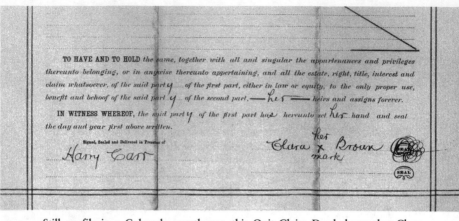

TO HAVE AND TO HOLD *the same, together with all and singular the appurtenances and privileges thereunto belonging, or in anywise thereunto appertaining, and all the estate, right, title, interest and claim whatsoever, of the said part y of the first part, either in law or equity, to the only proper use, benefit and behoof of the said part y of the second part.——her——heirs and assigns forever.*

IN WITNESS WHEREOF, *the said part y of the first part has hereunto set her hand and seal the day and year first above written.*

Signed, Sealed and Delivered in Presence of

Harry Carr

Clara X Brown
mark

Still on file in a Colorado courthouse, this Quit Claim Deed shows that Clara signed documents with an X, a legal signature for those who could not spell their names.

name, was marking her "X" on legal mining documents.

This was called "grubstaking." A miner could concentrate his energy on gold-digging when he knew his "grub" and his lodging were taken care of. Clara agreed to grubstake several mines, including the Argentine, the OK, and the Red, White and Blue, all of which belonged to Jerry and Lorenzo.

When these miners discovered a lode of gold or silver, Clara got her share of the profits. To Clara's great surprise, many of these mines starting paying off. Money, lots and lots of it, began rolling in. Clara used that money as a nest egg. She invested it so it would make more money. She soon was buying houses and land in the area—signing deeds as well as mining claims.

Although some people would have taken their money and flaunted their wealth, buying elegant clothes or a fancy home,

Clara did not. She kept her same cabin with its chilly outhouse, and hung her cotton aprons on the same old wall nails. She had more important purchases to be saving for.

She knew that Jacob Adriance's plan for building the Methodist church would be expensive, so she began to squirrel money away for the new church. She was also saving for trips. If Eliza didn't show up in Central, Clara fully intended to travel all through the streets and countryside of the nation, anywhere and everywhere, until she found her.

Pretty soon, people in Central City were calling Clara an "angel." How did she know to appear just when a person was reaching for a helping hand? In this hurry-up town, Clara was the one a newcomer would search out if he needed a good word, a bit of mothering, or a hearty chuckle. Laughing at jokes, gabbing about the "crimpy" weather, Aunt Clara would chat up a storm until it was time for her to move on to another neighbor or get back to her laundry work. To Clara, nothing was so valuable—not time, not money, not love—that it couldn't be given away to someone who needed it more.

Within days after arriving, Clara had made more money washing shirts than she'd ever seen in her life. Within a year, she owned real estate and mining claims in Central City, Georgetown, Denver, Idaho Springs, and Boulder. Now she had her nest egg, and her wealth was growing day by day. Within ten years, Clara would have ten thousand dollars.

Panhandlers and cardsharps called that kind of fortune "Lady Luck." Clara called it God's grace. Whatever it was called, Aunt Clara Brown, ex-slave and laundress, was on her way to becoming one of the richest women in the West.

How to Launder and Press Gold Miners' Shirts

You need: two buckets, two laundry tubs, a metal boiler tank, a washboard, lye soap, water, a knife, clothespins, rope, wood, a flat-topped stove, an iron, and strong muscles.

String the rope from a nail on the outside of your house, then loop it around a pine tree and back again.

Place your boiler on the stove.

Fetch water in your buckets from the creek, since there is no running water. Get enough to fill one washtub and your boiler.

Strike a match to light the wood fire in the stove. Fill your boiler with water.

Slice your bar of lye soap into thin pieces. Toss the pieces into the boiler water and stir, until it's nice and soapy.

When the water is hot, use a bucket to transfer it to your empty washtub. Put the shirts in.

One at a time, rub the wet shirts on the washboard, concentrating on the dirtiest spots. Keep rubbing until the shirts are clean and fresh-smelling.

Rinse each shirt in the rinse tub.

Wring each shirt by hand, squeezing hard to get the water out.

Hang each damp shirt on the line; fasten it with extra clothespins, so the wind won't whip it off.

When all the shirts are washed, dump your washtubs.

Go get more water in your buckets from the creek, and rinse out your tubs and boiler.

Hang the washboard and bucket up in a tree to dry.

While the clothes are drying, heat your iron on the stovetop.

Take the shirts off the line and drop them in a basket.

Lay each shirt on top of a cloth on your kitchen table and use the heavy, hot iron to press out the wrinkles.

Fold the ironed shirts and put them into your laundry basket.

Carry the basket on your head, up and down the mountain trails, delivering the clean, pressed clothes to your customers.

15

All That Glitters

One of the countless folk who came knocking on Clara's door in Central City was an elegantly dressed Negro gentleman, fresh off a wagon from Chicago. Barney Ford was his name, and he'd been told to look her up, since he was interested in mining, and needed a place to stay. As well-to-do as Barney was, he could not—since he was a Negro—rent a hotel room or a cabin. He was not ready to buy a home or build his own cabin right away, so his only other alternatives were to either camp out in a tent or ask Clara Brown for temporary lodging.

It was the spring of 1860, and Clara welcomed Barney to stay in her woodshed. Now she and Henry Poynter had company for supper every evening, and storytelling by the fire every night. What stories Barney had to tell! Before running away, he'd been a slave on his master's Mississippi riverboat. With the help of an actor aboard, Barney had turned his face pink with greasepaint. Disguised as "Miss Cora May," in a lovely blue dress and bonnet, Barney had sashayed right off his master's boat to freedom. From there, he'd been helped into a fancy carriage and hustled through the Underground Railroad.

Night after night, Clara listened to stories like the ones she'd heard back in Leavenworth. Barney had traveled from one red-kerchiefed conductor to the next—by boat, wagon, barge, carriage, and on foot. Once, he was even stashed in a casket with a few holes poked in the side for air, and taken by hearse all the way to Chicago. A freedom fighter named H. O. Wagoner met him there.

Soon after, Barney had fallen in love with Henry Wagoner's sister Julia, and married her. Successful ventures in the hotel industry had enabled Barney to invest in a new project—gold-mining. He planned to strike it rich, then go home to Chicago to give Julia the fine life she deserved.

Henry was Barney's business partner, and would be soon joining him here in Gold Country—one more ex-slave for Clara to befriend. Together, these two brilliant and literate men would later change history as politicians, delaying Colorado from claiming statehood until it guaranteed Negroes the right to vote.

Clara told Barney she was thinking of taking all her savings and heading back east to search for Eliza. Hold off,

Barney suggested. He was convinced that Abraham Lincoln would win the election that year. If so, civil war would be probably declared shortly after his 1861 inauguration. If Clara waited until the war ended, and slavery was abolished nationwide, her trip would be safer than trying to travel during these tumultuous times.

It turned out that Barney was right. The animosity that had been building for years between the Southern states and the Northern states now came to a head. Slavery was just one of many factors that caused civil war to break out in April of 1861. That spring, Central City cleared out as miners by the droves enlisted in the army. Lorenzo Bowman went to fight with the colored regiment of Union army volunteers. By far, the majority of argonauts were pro-Union, so most of them went off to fight for the North.

Southern sympathizers were suddenly unwelcome in Denver and Central City, and had to go into hiding. Even the revered gold miner William Green Russell was taunted for his opinions, and was forced to move back to his Georgia home, where he fought for the Confederacy.

In hideaways in the mountains, in backrooms in the towns, Confederate plots were in the making. Most Southerners out west considered Negroes to be an inferior race of people, born for a single purpose: to serve as slaves to whites. Whenever they could get away with it, they waged their own private war on colored residents. They harassed, tortured, and even went as far as murdering local Negroes.

Barney Ford was one of their first targets. After staying with Clara for a few weeks, he had staked out a mining claim to search for gold, and built his own cabin in the mountain town of Breckenridge. One night, a band of white miners broke in and threatened him at gunpoint, demanding that he vacate the property immediately. Didn't Barney know that the area he and Lorenzo and Jeremiah were working was disparagingly nicknamed "Nigger Hill"? They told him that "niggers" couldn't own mining claims, and they were claiming his cabin and the land for themselves.

Barney escaped with only the clothes on his back, and headed down to Denver to rethink his plan. Legally, Negroes were not barred from owning mine claims, but in the mountains, guns were often the final law. Clara had been smart in keeping all her purchases quiet, so that no white men had the opportunity to object to a "colored" woman owning property.

Clara herself caught a hostile glance now and then, mostly from recently arrived miners who didn't know her. Clara's practice was to ignore the bullies. She knew that confrontation with a gun-slinging frontiersman, often with a bellyful of whisky, was dangerous.

However, Clara was a well-loved and integral member of the mountain community now. No shrinking violet, when verbally assaulted on the street, she spoke out. The *Central*

City Miners Register wrote about one of her reports:

——We are in receipt of a communication from Gld Aunt Clara, than whom there is not a more respectable unpright colored woman in the territory, in which she compiains of some very indecent, disgraceful and insulting language addressed to her on one of our streets by some low-lived fellow who considers himself far her superior. We have only to say that it is never honorable fur a big boy to pick on a little boy, or one who claims to be the superior to insult his inferior. No gentleman will do it. Whenever we hear of an attempt on the part of rowdies to maliciously injure any one, whether black or white, no matter how low down in the scale of society: we put down the rowdies as lower than those they attempt to injure. In the days of slavery in the south he who would so injure a slave was sure at once to be made to feel the penalties of the law. We mention these things because we have heard of several like instances of late, and they are cetainly disgraceful to any community.

Although the animosity of the Civil War was felt in Clara's area, argonauts were spared the bloody battles that devastated the East. Instead, much closer to Clara, a different war was brewing. Friendly relations with the Arapaho and Cheyenne were deteriorating.

In 1861, Congress had established Kansas as a state and Colorado as a territory. The Colorado Territorial army had tricked the Arapaho into signing still another new treaty. Called the Fort Wise Treaty, it was negotiated by Albert Boone, the grandson of Daniel Boone, the Wilderness Road pioneer. It forced the Indians to move out of Denver, and confined them to a place about 150 miles away, not far from the Starvation Trail that Clara had traveled two years before. Settlers called the area Sand Creek. The Indians called it "the land of no water."

Three Arapaho chiefs, including Little Raven, had signed the treaty without permission from the rest of the tribe. Conflict followed. By now, the Indians' simple life had been ravaged. Buffalo were scarce, so food was hard to come by. So was clothing. The Indians wore whatever they found, stole, or were given: sunbonnets, frilly skirts, army jackets, miner shirts. Foreign diseases like cholera had been carried in by argonauts and were killing off members of the tribe.

Rebels within the tribe were angry, and had no intention of honoring a treaty signed dishonestly. With so many key army men gone off to the Civil War, the Indian renegades saw a perfect chance to retaliate. They began breaking into pioneers' homes to regularly steal food, clothing, and horses.

Settlers were terrified and outraged. To get even, the

army cut off all supplies of food, medicines, and arms that they'd been giving to the Indians. William Byers fanned the flames. "It is time the redskins learned to behave themselves," he wrote in his *Rocky Mountain News*. "They are paving the way for extermination faster than nature requires."

What about the treaties, with their glittering promises of land and protection for the Arapaho and Cheyenne? The old treaties had been written, signed, broken. New treaties were written, signed, broken. Then, in June of 1864, catastrophe struck.

The Hungates, a family of white farmers, were found murdered by Indians outside their cabin. Scalped and mutilated, the bodies of the parents and two little girls were pulled from the well they'd been thrown in, and put on display in Denver. Another war was about to break out, this time a war waged on Clara's friends: the Arapaho and Cheyenne.

"Necktie Parties"

Was there law and order in Central City? There was no order, but there was swift law. If someone was accused of murder, the trial took place on the spot. No waiting in jail, no spending time finding a good attorney, no wasting paper on jury-duty notices. The accused was dragged into any local saloon with enough space for a trial. The jury was picked from the customers—anyone not too drunk to make a rational decision could be chosen as a juror.

Public hanging was the penalty for murder or horse-stealing. Territorial "hanging judge," Isaac Parker, had no mercy, they said. Not only did he order death sentences, but if local authorities were too busy to carry out sentencing, then Parker hanged the culprits himself.

During Clara's stay in Central City, eighty-eight men and seven women were hanged. Crowds gathered to watch, with picnics spread out. Executioners would sometimes string a white sheet behind the criminal for better visibility. Clara steered clear of the "necktie parties." They only brought back grim memories of the hanging stories of her slave days.

The Word of the Lord

Clara's friend Jacob Adriance often stayed in her woodshed when he hiked up the mountain, carrying the word of the Lord to Central City. He walked from one mining settlement to the next, sometimes all the way to Denver and back, preaching sermons. Reverend Adriance walked so much that he spent more money on moccasins than on food!

The minister who presided over the whole Rocky Mountain Methodist Church was John Milton

Chivington. Although he and Clara were not close friends, she went to hear his fiery sermons, which drew huge crowds when he visited Central City. Chivington was nicknamed the "Fighting Parson" because his bigoted Missouri congregation had threatened his life if he continued to preach anti-slavery sermons. To protect himself, he spoke from the pulpit armed with two pistols.

As much as he hated slavery, Chivington showed no brotherly love for the local Indians when he arrived in Denver. "It simply is not possible for Indians to obey or even understand any treaty," he told a group of church deacons in 1864. "I am fully satisfied, gentlemen, that to kill them is the only way we will ever have peace and quiet in Colorado."

CHAPTER 16

Hikomini

The years of 1864 and 1865 were hard on Clara. For one thing, settlers had gambled on Cherry Creek staying as bone-dry as it had been when they first came west. Both Byers's newspaper and the city hall had been built on stilts in the middle of the creek bed. All Denver's important legal papers were locked in a safe in the city offices. In May of 1864, a quick thaw melted the mountain snows, sending water rushing down the slopes. Cherry Creek overflowed. Waist-deep, gushing water toppled the building. It flooded streets, homes, and businesses. Clara's real-estate records were washed away, ink streaming down the pages until they were unreadable.

Ownership of real estate was only as good as the paper it was written on. With no machines to copy crucial papers, there was no way to prove who owned what. Claim-jumping was as popular as ever. The biggest, fastest guns quickly took over the best property. Clara lost all her claims in Denver: claims she'd hoped to sell to pay for her trip to find Eliza Jane.

This was difficult news for Clara, but the worst was still to come. Financial losses were far less important to her than human losses. Fear struck her heart when she heard reports that surfaced in August of 1864.

The Colorado military had decided to raise a regiment to stop the Indian "problem" once and for all. Since Fort Leavenworth was still the headquarters for the western army, officials asked Governor Evans of Kansas for permission to proceed. The governor in turn needed clearance from his

A photograph of the devastating Denver flood of 1864. Twelve people died in the flash flood, and bits of type from Byers's news office could still be found in Cherry Creek a century later.

superiors in Washington, D.C. Had the military tried every last possible way to make peace with the Indians? Washington officials wanted to know. Yes, Evans told them. All treaty attempts had failed. In that case, Washington conceded.

On August 12, Clara's friends read her the full-page ad that ran in the *Central City Register*. ATTENTION! INDIAN FIGHTERS! it announced. Any men in Colorado who hadn't gone off to fight the Civil War were invited to join a volunteer cavalry in a war against the Indians. The soldiers would work for one hundred days, from September 28 to December 28. They would be trained, outfitted, and paid—and could keep "all horses and other plunder taken from the Indians."

This was tragic news for Clara, but welcome news for the miners in the mountain towns. Winter was coming, and most of them would be trekking down to Denver to wait out the snowstorms. They might as well make some money, get fed regularly, and protect their fellow argonauts at the same time. All the cavalry positions were filled within days.

Colonel Chivington was appointed to lead the army. Colonel John Chivington? Clara knew him as Reverend Chivington, the Methodist minister whose shirts she laundered and whose church she supported with hard-earned funds. She'd heard him share the word of God, but she'd also heard him preach disdain for the "red savages." He believed that extermination of the Indians was the only way to bring peace to the Gold Country.

Clara had never understood Chivington's hatred for her

Indian friends. He was always kind and helpful to her, and vigorously outspoken about the immorality of slavery. Would he have treated her differently, she wondered, if he knew she was part Cherokee? She was astonished to discover Chivington was so convinced that he'd been called to a godly mission that he had temporarily quit his church work to join the army.

Governor Evans was pleased to have Chivington, such a committed and unyielding man, in charge. "Kill all hostile Indians," Evans decreed. At the same time, Evans invited any friendly Indians who wanted to keep the peace, to visit a nearby army fort. There, they would be given food and supplies. Word spread, and small groups of Indians, sick and starving, went. They were met by U.S. army guards and shot on sight.

Far from the line of battle, in her little cabin in the mountains, Clara did what she could. She invited friends for special prayer meetings. Huddled in the flickering firelight, they prayed for peace. They were grateful when September began with a spark of hope.

The Cheyenne and Arapaho chiefs heard about the volunteer cavalry. In desperation, they asked their army friends Captain Silas Soule, Major Edward Wynkoop, and Lieutenant Joe Cramer to set up a parlay. Over the years, they had learned to trust these men, who had always been true to their word. The Indians had one goal—to speak face to face with Colonel Chivington and Governor Evans, so they could arrive at an agreement that would stop the bloodshed once and for all.

In September, Black Kettle, White Antelope, Left Hand,

Little Raven, and other chiefs rode into Denver with their tribes. They set up tents and tepees at nearby Camp Weld, where Evans had agreed to meet them. The Indians camped out for weeks, waiting for the army officials to appear.

Chivington and Evans, however, were no longer in a position to discuss peace. They had assured their superiors in Washington that they had already exhausted all hopes of nonviolent settlement. If they sat down now to negotiate, they'd look inept. If a peaceful agreement was reached, there'd be no need for their expensive hundred-day army, and Evans could be replaced for his poor judgment.

Cheyenne and Arapaho leaders pose with their white army friends at the Camp Weld Council, 1864. Major Edward Wynkoop (left) and Captain Silas Soule (right) are the two men kneeling in front. Cheyenne Chief Black Kettle is seated directly behind Wynkoop.

Besides, they had both long ago labeled Soule, Wynkoop, and Cramer as "Injun lovers"—officials with white skin and Indian hearts, who were far too willing to listen to the "savages" and give them land and arms and supplies.

Chivington and Evans finally showed up, simply to inform the chiefs that all the treaties had failed. Stubbornly, they refused to discuss further agreements. The Indians packed up and went back to their winter camp at Sand Creek.

By now, it was fall and Central City was already white with snow. As she and her mammy had done every autumn, Clara prepared well for the coming winter. She stacked firewood in her shed, she stored fruit jams and pickled vegetables in tightly capped jars, and she beat the dust out of woolen blankets to hang on the north wall. Her wooden shelves were stocked with jerky she had dried, and she bought extra fuel and matches for the smoky black kerosene lamp that lit her cabin when the sun went down.

Clara knew that most of her Indian friends were not so well prepared. Buffalo were scarce these days, and nearly all their food and warm clothing had always come from the buffalo. In just a few short years, the Indians had begun to rely almost entirely on soldiers for all their needs, as slaves relied on their masters. With peace talks breaking down, surely the army had no intention of supplying even the friendly Indians for the winter.

Clara was torn. Should she pack up some goods and head down to Denver, finding a way to travel out to the barren flatland of Sand Creek? Her mountain friends warned her that it would be too dangerous. She should not attempt to get into the middle of an escalating war. The Indians may be ill and starving, but the government had promised them protection as long as they stayed at Sand Creek. Her friends there would surely, at the very least, be safe from attack. Clara stayed put, and continued her prayer meetings.

Now it was November 1864. To Clara's Cheyenne friends, November was Hikomini, the Month of the Freezing Moon. An early storm had hit Sand Creek, and snow glittered in the moonlight like a blanket of frozen stars. Inside their tepees, the Arapaho and Cheyenne sucked on stewed rawhide ropes and moccasin leather to stave off starvation. As expected, the soldiers had not provided them with supplies this year. They were lucky to find an occasional rabbit or deer or dog to give them food and clothing.

In Denver, Chivington had now finished training his hundred-day volunteer cavalry. Convinced that the Sand Creek Indians were hostile Arapaho and Cheyenne who had killed the Hungate family, and convinced that they would keep on killing innocent white settlers, Chivington decided his troops would stage a surprise attack.

Several of the officers, including Soule, Wynkoop, and Cramer, were appalled. They knew that the Sand Creek people were not hostile Indians. They were friendly, and weakened, and had been promised military protection for the winter. Nevertheless, the army officers had sworn to follow orders, and they prepared their regiments to go.

Sand Creek was a vast and remote prairieland, and Chivington wasn't sure where to find the settlement. The best man to lead the troops was Jim Beckwourth, the mountain scout from the trading post in Denver. Known as Medicine Calf to the Indians, and having befriended the local Cheyenne, he knew exactly how to find them. Some people believe that, like those of many scouts, Beckwourth's loyalties could be bought for a price. Others believe that Chivington forced him against his will.

It was Thanksgiving Day. While Clara was sharing a meal with her friends in the mountains, seven hundred soldiers set out from Denver. His huge bowie knife at his side, Beckwourth led them through deep snow for three days. A second guide, Robert Brent, whose brothers lived at the Sand Creek camp, was forced by Chivington to betray his own family and help find the exact location.

The soldiers descended on the village at dawn on the twenty-ninth of November, surprising the Indians. Immediately, the Cheyenne and Arapaho ran out, waving white flags in surrender. Many of the soldiers had never seen an Indian settlement, and expected well-armed chiefs in warpaint to defend the attack. What they saw was a village of frightened, downtrodden people with no visible weapons. Most were women and children.

Chivington's men attacked anyway. Captain Soule defied his superior's orders. Seeing the flags of surrender and the ragged state of the Indians he knew so well, he refused to allow his regiment to fight. They sat on horseback and watched while Chivington's troops, in six hours, slaughtered nearly two hundred innocent people.

The next day, while his army was camped in the blood-spattered snow by Sand Creek, Chivington sat down with pen and paper. He wrote this letter to his commanding officer in Fort Leavenworth, exaggerating his victory:

In the last 10 days, my command has marched 300 miles, 100 of which the snow was two feet deep. After a march of 40 miles last night I, at daylight this morning, attacked a Cheyenne village of 130 lodges, from 900 to 1,000 warriors strong; killed Chiefs Black Kettle, White Antelope, Knock Knee and Little Robe, and between 400 and 500 other Indians, and captured as many ponies and mules. Our loss [was] 9 killed, 38 wounded. All did nobly. Think I will catch some more of them 80 miles [away], on Smoky Hill. Found white man's scalp, not more than three days old, in one of the lodges.

> *J. M. Chivington*
> *Colonel, Commanding,*
> *First District of Colorado*
> *And First Indian Expedition*

News of Sand Creek reached Clara on a cold night in early December. Jerry Lee's wife, Emily, read to her from the *Miners' Register,* which ran the headline: THE INDIANS WHIPPED. Nearly all the Indians Clara had ever met, even the chiefs who had tried so hard to make peace, were reported dead.

Just before Christmas, the hundred-day troops marched back to Denver to celebrate their victory. They paraded up and down the streets, cheered on by throngs of pioneers who were jubilant that the Indians had been defeated. With a live eagle on a pole in his hand, Chivington led the march. His soldiers carried their trophies on sticks: severed Cheyenne fingers and bloody Arapaho scalps.

The crowds saluted, proud of their victorious volunteer regiment. The celebration moved from one saloon to another, and lasted for days. The soldiers had taken no prisoners except for three young children who were put on display at a downtown theater, surrounded by scalps taken from their families. Newspaper publisher Byers made posters announcing the spectacle, and people paid admission to gawk at the Indian children.

Soule and Cramer wrote powerful letters of protest about the attack, which Wynkoop secretly delivered to officials in Washington, D.C. Within days, federal authorities headed to Denver to investigate. When they heard testimony from soldiers who had been at the massacre, they set up an official hearing in Washington. The testimony told a story very different from what people had been told at the Christmas festivities, very different from the letter Chivington had sent to his superior. They confirmed the atrocities that Soule had described in his letter:

"It was hard to see little children on their knees have

their brains beat out by men professing to be civilized. One squaw was wounded and a fellow took a hatchet to finish her. She held her arm up to defend herself and he cut one arm off and held the other with one hand and dashed the hatch through her brain."

Captain Soule himself did not get a chance to finish telling his side of the story, because on April 24 he was killed, shot in the back on Lawrence Street in Denver. By the time the hearings had ended, Chivington was stripped of his positions both in the army and in the Methodist Church. Many soldiers wanted to see Chivington hanged. Instead, with no apology and no remorse, he simply packed up and went back to Nebraska. An army judge stated publicly that Sand Creek was "a cowardly and cold-blooded slaughter, sufficient to cover its perpetrators with indelible infamy and the face of every American with shame and indignation."

Soon after the massacre, the war pipe was lit by the Cheyenne leaders. Since peace with the white settlers had not succeeded, the only choice open to them, they agreed, was revenge. Even though most of Clara's Indian friends who survived were moved to reservations in Oklahoma and Wyoming, bands of braves wreaked havoc in Colorado. With renewed fury, they robbed, attacked, and burned forts and homes and stagecoaches.

The Indians' wars had only just begun. Clara was heartsick.

Extermination

Several soldiers and civilians, remorseful after the massacre, became ardent supporters of Indian rights. Yet even after the Sand Creek tragedy, most local pioneers had few qualms about white settlers killing Indians. There was talk of a new method that wasn't as messy as bloody shootings: poisoning. In Minnesota, a group of pioneers had saturated boxes of bread with strychnine, and left the food on the road for the Indians to eat.

The Miners' Register *of Central City ran an article about the strychnine poisonings. "That is the kind of warfare we approve of, and should be glad to see it introduced here. It is cheaper," the article said, "than to kill them with powder and lead, and . . . fully as effective."*

CHAPTER 17

No More Hundred Lash for Me

In April of 1865, when Clara heard the Civil War was over, she was ecstatic. The North had won, and to most Negroes that meant one thing: the end of slavery. She ran into the streets with her neighbors, rejoicing, singing, and sobbing with relief.

Barney Ford had advised that she delay her all-out search for Eliza Jane until the war ended. Now she was certain she could make plans to pack up and set out on her big journey back to Kentucky.

Only ten days later, on Wednesday, April 19, all the emergency whistles in the stamp mills shrieked at once, sending their piercing alarms through town. Clara dropped her laundry in a pile and rushed to the newspaper office. There was shocking news. On April 14, President Abraham Lincoln had been assassinated!

Men went out to knock on every cabin door to sadly

announce a day of mourning. All of Central City came to an immediate halt. Clara closed her laundry, the mines sent their workers home, and the churches opened their doors.

This gaunt, sunken-eyed president had been a hero to Clara, and she was stunned by the news of his death. Even so, she was taken aback by the depth of grief she saw in her friends and neighbors. Some wept uncontrollably, as if their entire worlds had come to an end.

Clara knew that two years ago, in 1863, Lincoln's Emancipation Proclamation had freed about three million slaves. Now he had lived to see the Civil War end with a Union victory. Didn't his good work mean that the rest of the slaves were free, and that all Negroes now had the same rights as white people?

No, it did not, Clara learned, as she listened to the eulogy and the personal declarations at church that day. The victory of the North only meant that the country was united. In many states, slavery was still legal, Negroes still could not vote, and non-whites still couldn't ride in public vehicles. It would take time for laws to be drawn up, and passed, and enforced.

How much time, Clara wanted to know. She was sixty-five years old now, and Eliza would be in her forties. How much more patience could she possibly have left in her aching heart?

Along with all the townspeople, Clara prayed fervently. She prayed that the politicians in Washington, D.C., would not slow the progress of the work Lincoln had begun. She prayed that his death would not stop the movement to bring freedom and equality to all people.

As Clara walked back to her cabin that day, she was truly anguished. She contemplated her whole situation. Her nest egg had been consistently accumulating more wealth. Her laundry business was booming. Her mining claims paid gold every time the men she'd grubstaked hit pay dirt. She now owned houses in Central City, mines in Idaho Springs, and property in Georgetown and Boulder.

Her home was still the safe little log cabin with its open door for disheartened prospectors. Her Methodist congregation had 225 members, and a new church building was being erected for which Clara had given more money than any other person. She'd helped other congregations, too, by donating funds to the Episcopal, Baptist, Catholic, and Presbyterian groups in town. But what good was all this success if she couldn't share it with Eliza Jane?

She'd heard how the war had left plantations burned, Southerners penniless, and many slaves on their own. The country was in chaos. Clara suspected that all those travel restrictions on colored people may have eased off. She figured people were far too busy reconstructing their shattered lives right now to worry about throwing Negroes off wagons and stagecoaches.

Her friends at church urged her to wait to travel until the Thirteenth Amendment to the Constitution was passed. It might take a month, maybe six months, and then slavery would be legally abolished, so she could count on a safer trip.

Clara couldn't wait. She sold some of her property and got enough cash to add to her savings to go back to the old homestead in Russellville, Kentucky. Perhaps the Brown sisters had heard news from Eliza. If they hadn't, she planned to travel the countryside by coach or on foot, until she was satisfied that she'd done all she could to reunite with her daughter.

In October of 1865, Clara shut down her laundry and set out back across the plains. The stagecoach for the crossing left from Denver. Clara paid for her tickets, first from Central City to Denver, then from Denver to Kansas City, and nobody gave her any trouble. She was on her way!

When she arrived in Denver, nothing looked familiar. Although she'd heard that the city had burned to the ground in 1863, she had never actually seen the devastation. Now it was already a far more beautiful place than the hodgepodge settlement of 1859. Sturdy new buildings, three and four stories tall, made of stone and brick, lined Larimer Street. Horses trotted along, pulling fancy coaches, and few covered wagons were in sight.

As the stagecoach pulled out of Denver, Clara caught herself looking for Cheyenne and Arapaho tepees, and felt a sadness all over again, even though she'd known they were long gone. Passing near Sand Creek felt ghostly. Out on the plains, small towns had cropped up, and very few buffalo herds grazed in the grasses.

Indians weren't the only threat on the trails anymore. Outlaws of every sort knew that coaches often carried gold to the river towns. Lying in wait for stagecoaches to pass, they held them up at gunpoint and robbed the passengers and drivers.

The outlaws had plenty of stagecoaches to choose from, since they ran regularly across the Great Plains now, with stage stops about every twelve miles. Although the seats were plush red velvet and the coaches handsome, the ride wasn't the most comfortable. Butterfield Overland Despatch now owned the company that used to belong to Russell, Majors and Waddell, and they crammed people in like sardines. The joke was that a passenger didn't pay for a seat, but for fifteen inches of space. Built for ten or twelve people, the coaches sometimes carried fifteen, forcing some passengers to ride on the hard middle bench, which was supposed to be a footrest.

Clara was relieved when she could get off for the evening and stretch her cramped legs and arms. Even so, it was luxurious compared with the wagon train. She didn't have to cook or launder or sleep outside through dust storms and downpours. At each stage stop, the passengers were fed, and they slept in blankets on the large cabin floor. Clara's stage made it through safely to Kansas City, in about twelve days. She then boarded a Union Pacific train to Russellville. It was the first time she'd set foot on the famous "iron horse," and she heard that plans were in the works for train tracks to be laid all the way to Denver soon.

When Clara arrived in Russellville, she walked the tree-lined streets straight to the rambling white house that was so familiar from her slave days. Mary Prue Brown and her husband, Richard Higgins, were shocked to see old Auntie Clara at their door, after six long years. They invited her to stay in their home, in the servants' quarters, as long as she'd like. The Higginses did everything they could to help Clara.

They wrote letters to local church ministers and postmasters, asking them to display information about Eliza Jane. They tried to track down everyone who might possibly have news. Valentine Cook, Clara's past minister in Logan County, had died years before. The Covingtons had moved. None of the churches or post offices found any records of a woman named Eliza Jane.

What about Spotsylvania County, Virginia? Clara wondered. Eliza might have gone there, thinking her mammy may have returned to her childhood home. Months later, they received a reply saying that all the county-court records had been destroyed in the Civil War.

What next? Just as Clara was mulling over her next move, in December of 1865, good news came. The Thirteenth Amendment had been ratified! The news sent Clara and the Higginses out into the streets, jumping for joy. Every slave across the nation was free! If Eliza Jane had not been manumitted already, today and forever, she was a free woman!

Rejuvenated by the excitement, Clara moved on. Her own mammy and her grandparents had been born "away down in

Tennessee." Free and independent, and perhaps looking for Clara, would Eliza head that way? Clara boarded a southbound train to Gallatin, and winter turned to spring as she hiked the Tennessee highways and byways. She stayed in tents and cabins with other Negroes, and they showered her with the warm hospitality she was used to giving.

What Clara saw along the way broke her heart. Freed slaves wandered along the roads, searching for their long-lost families, and for work. They had walked away from plantations and big houses and cramped slaves' quarters, and headed for states where they hoped there was no hatred for them. All they owned were the clothes on their backs, the tattered shoes on their feet, and perhaps a few treasures in their ragbags.

Clara of all people knew what they were feeling. She remembered the confusion she felt when she was finally freed at fifty-six years of age. Her heart went out to those folks who were at the same time brimming with hope and starving for a meal.

Everywhere Clara went, former slaves wandered, but Eliza Jane was not among them. Every day she woke up with hope, thinking this might be the reunion day she'd been waiting for. Every night she prayed not to be discouraged. After several months with no news, she seemed to be at journey's end.

How many times could her heart break before it was too much? One night she fell to her knees, weeping and praying. God's voice, as always, came to her in her hour of need. Clara felt that God was telling her to put together a "family" of freed slaves who had no kinfolk, and invite them back to Colorado with her. She could pay for their trips, find jobs for them, and get them places to stay until they got on their feet.

After all, she not only had spiritual strength and fortitude, but now she also possessed earthly resources. She had money. She had land. She even had a few homes. Since she had not found her own flesh-and-blood daughter, she could instead adopt other sons and daughters who couldn't find their families, either.

God spoke, and Clara listened. All the details fell into place within days. Among the thousands of wandering ex-slaves, Clara had met a man named Jackson Smith. Clara's mother had told her stories of slave life in Tennessee, and from Jackson's description of his childhood, it seemed as if he could very well be her nephew. Clara invited him to go back to Colorado with her, and he was thrilled.

As she and Jackson headed to Leavenworth to plan a wagon train, Clara gathered more ex-slaves from Tennessee and Kentucky who wanted to travel with them. Soon she'd brought along about twenty adoptees, as many as she could afford to take back.

By the time they reached Leavenworth, Clara's old church had somehow gotten the news about her traveling "family." They welcomed the group warmly, giving everyone a place to stay while they organized their trip.

Clara went to an outfitter for expert help in planning the wagon train. There had to be room for everyone to ride and sleep on board. Nobody would be walking or sleeping outside, unless they wanted to. In three days, they were ready to go. On the final night, the congregation invited Clara's flock to a huge send-off celebration dinner.

The trip with this joyful bunch was a delight for Clara. They laughed around the nightly campfires. They sang the old slave tunes they'd once sung in secret, like "Many Thousand Go":

"No more peck o' corn for me, no more, no more . . .

No more driver's lash for me, no more, no more . . .

No more hundred lash for me, no more, no more . . .

Many thousand go."

Every step of the way was familiar to Clara: nooning, meals of "grease and beans," prairie-dog towns, Indian barters, snow, rain, scorching heat, and buffalo. This time, there were stage stops and small towns where they could refresh their supplies, making the death-defying Starvation Trail much easier. After another trek of eight weeks, they made it across the Great Plains.

"They arrived . . . happy and triumphant," the newspapers announced when they sang and danced their way into Denver in mid-July. Clara felt especially at peace. She had gone back to the green hills and the songbirds and the big white houses of Kentucky, where home had been for nearly fifty years of her life. Now the Rocky Mountains, with their dramatic weather, wild spirit, and independent pioneers, truly felt like home. Clara couldn't wait to show her new kinfolk the mountains and cool streams of Central City. She immediately traded her wagons and oxen in Denver and led her flock up the canyon.

There, they set up two big tents—one for the men, one for the women—until Clara could help them settle in with food, shelter, and clothing. The tents did not work out too well. Used to warm Southern weather, the former slaves nearly froze to death during the cold mountain nights, which can get bone-frigid even in summer. Clara had to harbor most of them in her cabin so they wouldn't become ill.

Who exactly did Clara bring back with her? How many people? Only Jackson Smith's name was recorded in a newspaper article. And the Denver and Central City newspapers all reported different numbers of people— somewhere between sixteen and thirty-four in all. One thing is certain: on that July day in 1866, when she led her new "family" home, the Negro population of Central City at least doubled.

Dazzled by Clara's thoughtful generosity, the mountain residents welcomed her back with open arms. What she'd done, they thought, was amazing, especially at the age of sixty-six! Fortunately for the newcomers, it looked as though there would be lots of job opportunities. Many people wanted to join in Clara's caring mission; they offered to hire Clara's newcomers to help with everything from housekeeping to mining.

The *Rocky Mountain News,* in an article entitled "A Woman in a Thousand," told readers the adventurous tale of how Clara "traveled through the length and breadth of Kentucky and Tennessee, gathering together her flock." Byers was full of praise. "We will put 'Aunt Clara' against the world, white or black," he wrote, "for industry, perseverance, energy, and filial love."

Disappearing Buffalo

The buffalo herds of the Great Plains, from Mexico to Canada, probably numbered over fifty million when Clara first journeyed west. It was common then to see herds from twenty to fifty miles in width. During Clara's lifetime, they were driven nearly to extinction.

Contests were run to see who could take the most buffalo hides in a year, and the numbers were staggering. Sometimes a single hunter killed 100 buffalo in a day, with one-man records set at 3,300 dead buffalo in one year.

When the Union Pacific railroad was built, between 1866 and 1870, the slaughter escalated. People in the East wanted to buy hides, and trains were an easy way to ship them. In two years alone, between 1872 and 1874, the railroads shipped

*1,378,349 hides and 6,751,000 pounds of buffalo
meat. Within ten years, there were so few buffalo left
that, after 1885, the railroads no longer carried
shipments.*

CHAPTER 18

Peaks and Valleys

The next ten years were busy ones for Clara. She got her family all fixed up in houses and on plots of land she still owned from Central City to Georgetown, from Idaho Springs to Denver. In time, through word of mouth and newspaper articles, each one of them found work, in building or mining, housekeeping or gardening. A few did laundry, taught by the first and best washerwoman in town, Clara herself.

Once she was confident that everybody was firmly settled, Clara took a look at her finances. Something, she discovered, was very wrong. It seemed she was missing a significant amount of her savings. She consulted a lawyer, who examined all her receipts and papers from the Kentucky trip.

He had bad news, he told her. She'd been swindled. Somewhere on her trip, Clara had been robbed of nearly four thousand dollars! It turned out that, back in Leavenworth, when

Clara had planned the wagon train, the outfitter had over-charged her and pocketed the extra money.

Still, Clara knew the Lord would provide. Her remaining financial holdings were many. She was one of the few women in Colorado who actually owned property, and the only Negro woman on record. By now she was known as one of the richest women in the West. By putting her savings to good use, "where moth and rust do not corrupt and where thieves do not break through and steal," she was certain her gains would always exceed her losses.

Unwilling to give up her search for Eliza Jane, Clara advertised a thousand-dollar reward for anyone who discovered her lost daughter. She paid to have letters sent to churches all over the country, announcing the reward. "The old lady . . . has firm faith in the efficacy of prayer," reported the *Denver Republican*. "She has never ceased to ask God . . . to restore her daughter to her."

Knowing that, for the time being, she had done all she could to find Eliza Jane, Clara felt it was time to plunge her hands into soapy water again, and get her business back on its feet. At home in the mountains, she flowed with the seasons. She knew that an early or late snow would be followed the next day by bright sunshine. She knew when to expect to hang shirts inside to avoid snow-laden clouds, and when she could string them outside in the fresh, crisp air. She awaited the sweet butterscotch scent of the ponderosa pines in the fall, and knew that their pollen would cover her shirts with a fine yellow dust if she left them out too long. She was growing older, and her life was peaceful.

Then, on an icy January night in 1873, Clara awoke to shouts outside her cabin. Wrapping her flannel robe around her, she hurried out the door. The streets were wild with panic, as flames leapt from the roof of St. Paul's Methodist Episcopal Church. *Fire!* It was the scariest imaginable word in the West, since every building was made of wood.

Her neighbors, racing across the frosty crust of snow, formed two lines. They cracked through the frozen layer of ice on the creek, filled buckets, and passed them up the line, tossing the water on the sky-high fire. Tall, wide flames swept from one side of Lawrence Street to the other, and one by one, buildings collapsed in a fiery wreck. By the time it was over, sixteen buildings had burned to the ground. Three of them were Clara's. The crowd, weary and numb with cold, dispersed without a word.

The next day, everyone gathered to talk about how to prevent such tragedy in the future. Did they need to organize a fire department? They all agreed it would be a wise idea. But right now, they had their hands full. President Ulysses S. Grant was visiting Central City in May, and there was no time to plan a fire department and plan for Grant's arrival at the same time.

This was the first time a president was paying an official visit to the Colorado mining towns, so everyone wanted to make a big impression. They planned to pave the street leading to his hotel, the Teller House, with gold bricks. But was gold special enough? After all, there was so much of it! Silver, the townspeople decided, was better, so they laid silver ingots smelted from the Caribou mine. Clara was there with the rest of the town to watch proudly as President Grant strode up the pure silver road worth twelve thousand dollars.

After Grant's departure, everybody got back to the business of mining, and the plan for the fire department was postponed. Then, one year later, in May of 1874, the worst happened. The whole business district went up in flames, burning Central City to ashes, including every piece of property Clara owned, except her own cabin.

This was financially devastating for Clara. By now she had cashed in and given away a great deal of her property. Still, she didn't despair. Every time one of her mines paid off, she invested the money in more land, or in more mining claims.

While Clara focused on her life in Central City, Barney Ford and H. O. Wagoner had traveled often to Washington, D.C., to fight for voting rights for all people of color in Colorado. They had finally won. In 1876, one hundred years after the signing of the Declaration of Independence, Colorado officially became a state. Every man of every color had the right to vote if they lived in the new Centennial State.

Over the years, Clara watched for a mail delivery every single day. Had anyone found Eliza? Her reward offer and her letter campaign had not brought in one word of encouragement. Nobody, it seemed, knew her daughter.

Then, in 1877, a possible ray of hope came Clara's way, this time from Kansas. Suddenly, Negroes by the thousands were moving to Wyandotte, a town near Kansas City, not far from Leavenworth. The newspapers said that Kansas had now become the site of the largest organized emigration of slaves who'd been freed after the Civil War.

The "bleeding" days in Kansas had left their scars. Because hundreds of people had been killed back in the 1850s, when the "Border Ruffians" and the "Red-Legs" were fighting over slavery, many pioneers had not felt safe about settling there. After the Civil War, there was plenty of land open, and hearing the news, thousands of ex-slaves poured into Kansas. Their steady exodus from the South to the dusty heartland of the country was remarkable. People began to call them "exodusters."

The exodus started one day in March of 1867, when a boatload of Negro passengers landed at the Wyandotte wharf. Each family had several children and a bag of personal belongings, but no money and no food. Not knowing where to go, they settled right there at the dock, out in the open, with no tents.

Within two weeks, nearly a thousand more impover-ished exodusters arrived. They had been persuaded by political scalawags in the South to go to Kansas, where, they'd been told, they'd receive a vote plus "forty acres of land and a mule." When the Negroes arrived, nothing was waiting for them. The promises were simply a way for those politicians to get rid of freed Negroes they didn't want around.

Clara heard that the citizens of Wyandotte had finally set up an area they called "Mississippi Town," where the Negroes could settle. The ex-slaves built houses out of whatever they could find—rubbish, tin cans, and paper. The only work available was in the dead of winter, when exodusters cut blocks of ice from the river. Without the means to support themselves, many died from starvation and disease.

John St. John, the new governor, formed a Relief Society. Newspapers across the nation told readers that volunteers were needed to give the exodusters medical care, food, and shelter. One article in April of 1879 was entitled "Call for Help."

An exoduster "town" in Kansas. Exodusters told the Kansas governor that life in the South was so cruel that they would rather die in the attempt to reach a better place than remain in the South any longer.

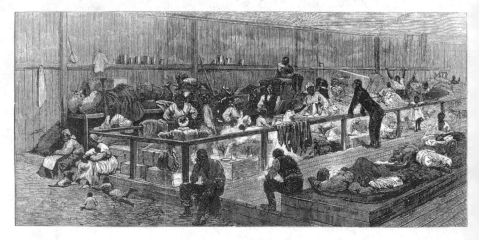

Thousands more refugees were on their way to Kansas by way of steamboat, it said, and they were arriving "in an entirely destitute condition . . . and are occupying the churches and public halls of that place."

Clara, no matter that she was now in her late seventies, was ever caring about folks in need. Besides, a familiar twinge was pulling at her heart. Since Eliza was not in Colorado, not in Tennessee, and not in Kentucky, wasn't there a good chance that she was among the Kansas exodusters?

Clara packed her bags. She was going to Kansas to help out. Her friends knew she planned to find Eliza Jane there, but they no longer encouraged her lifelong dream. Their hearts went out to poor Auntie Clara, who had hoped all her life for the impossible. What were the odds of her ever finding her daughter among millions of wandering exodusters? Clara's friends were westerners, betting folk, familiar with odds. After all these years, few would have put their money on Clara's dream of finding Eliza Jane. It was too much of a gamble.

The Great Locust Mystery

One July morning in 1874, when she stepped outside her cabin, Clara was attacked by flying insects. Millions of them swarmed in, forming huge buzzing clouds that darkened the sky. Their yellow-green guts smeared up windows, and their shells crackled under the soles of her shoes.

It turned out to be a swarm of Rocky Mountain locusts, which the Guinness Book of World Records *later called the "greatest concentration of animals" ever. "The swarm must have contained at least 12.5 trillion insects with a total weight of 27.5 million tons," it reported.*

The locusts flew out east to Nebraska and Kansas and attacked in swarms 150 miles wide and 100 miles long. They devoured entire crops, a hundred acres in an hour, and sucked the living right out of the farmers. They even stopped trains, clogging the wheels so that the heavy locomotives couldn't move. It was over a week before their numbers dwindled, and the swarms finally disappeared, as mysteriously as they had come.

"Pap" Singleton

For ten years straight, the numbers of Negro emigrants just kept growing. One man, Benjamin Singleton, a seventy-year-old who'd been a runaway slave, led a thousand freed slaves from Tennessee to Kansas. A carpenter and cabinetmaker, Singleton lived simply. Over the years he had saved all his money for only one goal—he dreamed of starting a colony of Negro people who would be independent and self-sustaining.

178

He used his savings to buy up all the land in Kansas he could afford. In 1877, Singleton began offering ex-slaves large pieces of his land for just five dollars. Word spread quickly through the Southern states, and Negroes began affectionately calling him the grandfatherly nickname of "Pap." Thousands headed out on foot, by boat, and by train to meet "Pap" in Kansas. In 1870, there were 17,108 Negroes in the state of Kansas. By 1880, the Negro population would swell to 43,107.

CHAPTER 19

A Genuine Barnacle

Clara left for Kansas in October of 1878, when the mountain peaks that stood fourteen thousand feet high along the Continental Divide were white with snow. Her stagecoach dropped her off at the Union Pacific Railroad station in Denver. Like the rest of the city, it was built of brick.

Once again, Clara barely recognized Denver. It had grown over the past decade into an elegant city. The brick and stone buildings were adorned with carved scrollwork, turreted roofs, and windows trimmed in intricate designs. Gaslights, which had replaced kerosene in 1871, glittered along Larimer Street and lit up the station.

Train travel was now a reality for Denverites, as the tracks carrying passengers and freight crossed the nation, from San Francisco to New York. The fact that the railway had been built at all was a miracle. Laying track all the way across the prairie took gargantuan amounts of funds, wooden ties, and workers. Indians had persistently ripped up the rails, in hopes of preserving their wide-open buffalo land.

This trip would take less than two days: no eight-week haul of trudging or wagon-bumping, no twelve days crammed into a bumpy stage that stopped twenty-five times on the way. There were luxuries: a bathroom on board, lamps in the cars, and velvet-cushioned seats with just two people to a bench.

Clara saw that there were many more towns than there'd been in 1865, and again, far fewer buffalo. She saw firsthand why the herds of the legendary buffalo were dwindling so quickly. Just outside Fort Hayes, the train slowed down, its metal wheels screeching to a halt. Excitement rippled through the cars. A herd of buffalo had been spotted!

Conductors hurried through the cars, passing out rifles to men and women, who rushed to the windows on one side of the train. They opened fire, whooping proudly each time they downed a buffalo. Clara had seen buffalo shot for sport on the wagon-train trail, but that had been nothing like this. One great beast fell after another, until the surviving herd stampeded off into the dust. The train chugged on, gaining speed until they were on their way again.

When Clara got off the train at Kansas City, she was introduced to Governor St. John. He was grateful for all the volunteers who had come from across the nation, and he personally greeted as many of them as he could. Clara handed him a special bag she'd carried from Colorado. It was money for the exodusters from Henry Reitze, from several churches in Denver and Central City, and from other friends. She was then escorted with other volunteers to Wyandotte.

There, fifty emigrants a day were dying! The poor people lay everywhere, their starving bodies just skin and

The Kansas Sufferers.

Aunt Clara Brown, whom everybody in Central knows, returned from a visit to Kansas some few days since, whither whither she went to look into the condition of the colored refugees, and in the interest of the sufferers generally. There are about 5,000 all told, and they are getting on as fast as could be expected. The greater portion have found employment, and the balance will, doubtless, in the course of time. Aunt Clara says they are an industrious and sober class of people, who only ask an opportunity to make an honest living. Their cry is work, work, and that is being given them as fast as possible. She was kindly received by Gov. St. John and the people generally. She thinks that in another year these people will be well to do and self-supporting.

The Reason.

bones. Clara rolled up her sleeves and got to the work she did best of all—nurturing. She tried to spoon food and liquids into the exodusters' parched mouths, to replenish their weak systems. She held those who were dying, and prayed over them. Months went by, and every day Clara saw some people die and some people gain back the strength to live.

The exodusters in Kansas had come mostly from Mississippi and Louisiana. Left sick and desolate from their long journeys, they were not strong enough to make the trip back to a harsh climate like Central City. Clara knew that when they began to heal, they would have a caring community of their own right by the Kaw River. Rather than invite them back with her, she would stay and care for them as long as they needed her.

Each time Clara wrapped a wound, she asked about Eliza. Each time she ladled soup into a bowl, she asked about Eliza. Sometimes, for a brief exhilarating moment, an exoduster would tell her that, yes, they did remember an Eliza Jane. But with more investigation, every time, it turned out not to be Clara's Eliza Jane.

Nearly a year went by. The condition of the exodusters began to stabilize, and Clara's hopes for ever reuniting with Eliza dwindled. In late summer, Clara returned home alone. A few days later, the *Central City Register-Call* of September 23, 1879, wrote:

> *Unfortunately, the long trip had taken its toll on Clara's health. She was nearly eighty, and she couldn't*

tramp around the country the way she had in her younger days. She had dropsy, which swelled up her feet and her hands, making it difficult to get around by the end of the day. Even worse, she had heart trouble. Whatever herb she had self-prescribed for her heart and her breathing wasn't working. She couldn't trudge up the steep streets delivering freshly ironed laundry anymore. She simply didn't have the breath to do it.

Her doctor prescribed morphine, a drug commonly used in Clara's time to treat heart disease. Although it took a patient's pain away, it could cause severe hallucinations and erratic behavior. What doctors did not realize was that it was a highly addictive drug. Clara took her doctor's advice and began to use morphine.

It turned out to be dangerous. Everyone in Central City had at one time or another seen Clara down on her knees, praying to thank God, or to praise God, or to ask for God's help. Since westerners didn't like to stick their noses in people's business, they took this habit to be endearing, simply "Auntie Clara's way." But now she started preaching from the top of her cabin roof, and her neighbors grew worried.

The morphine treatment was clearly far worse than Clara's disease. Her friends decided that something had to be done, and her doctor agreed. By 1880, Clara was too sick to survive another mountain winter. She needed to close down her laundry for good and move to Denver as soon as possible.

But Denver had gotten very expensive these past years. There were no more twenty-five-dollar cabins, as there had been back in 1859. Clara had made the decision years ago to spend her money on what she believed was worthwhile. For fifteen years now, not only had there been losses from fires and flood, but Clara had also been gradually selling off her mine holdings and her properties. Her funds had gone to support her family members, to build churches, and to pay for her trips to find her daughter. Old Aunt Clara was out of money.

Miracles seemed to be a natural part of Clara's life. Once again, something amazing happened. She was given a home in Denver, a cozy little white house on Arapaho Street. The anonymous donor promised that Clara could keep the home for the rest of her life.

Clara said good-bye to Central City, knowing that she would never return. Good-bye to the yellow aspens of autumn, the long winter snows, the heart-stopping steepness of the streets, the marmots, the pikas, the funny black squirrels. She was beginning a new chapter in her life. In 1880, she headed down to Denver.

A year later, just before Christmas, Clara received a letter on cream-colored stationery, telling her that she was now officially proclaimed a Member of the Colorado Pioneer Society. This was not only a great honor, but it also meant that every month for the rest of her life, she'd receive a small monthly pension to help her make ends meet. When the

Pioneer Society was first formed in 1872, its constitution limited members to "white male citizens who became residents prior to December 31, 1860."

Thanks to Barney Ford and Henry Wagoner, the bylaws had been changed in 1881. The word "white" was eliminated, and women were voted in as official "honorary" members. Clara was the only woman of color to be named an official Colorado pioneer—or "barnacle," as they were nicknamed.

Like barnacles stuck on a rock or to a boat, the pioneers were the ones who "stuck" out west when others were washed away. They persevered; they kept going when all seemed lost; they settled the land, and built homes and businesses. They believed they'd strike gold even while others laughed behind their backs. And Aunt Clara Brown was as true a barnacle as anyone could find anywhere.

The Iron Horse

In the 1870s, a steam engine called a locomotive pulled the train cars. Inside, men kept a firebox burning with wood, which in turn boiled water. The steam from the water flowed through metal pipes, creating enough energy to move a piston back and forth, making the wheels turn. The locomotive was loud and monstrous, belching out billows of smoke and steam across the countryside. The train would

*stop at Union Pacific stations along the way to pick
up more wood to refuel.*

Colorado Help

*When Clara was in Kansas, Coloradans back
home were trying to figure out how they could best
help the freed Negroes on a large scale. At a meeting
in May of 1879, the citizens decided that the state
"should endeavor to bring some of the emigrants to
Colorado and colonize them here." Ex-slaves were
leaving Kentucky, Tennessee, Virginia, and the
Carolinas by the droves. Highly trained as mechanics,
house servants, and farm hands, there were plenty of
places to hire these emigrants in Colorado. A plan
was put into place, and freed Negroes were invited to
journey to Denver, where they would be hired in the
city, or sent to public lands farther south to farm.*

CHAPTER 20

The Valentine

Not long after she moved into her little white house in Denver, sociable Aunt Clara was bedridden. She no longer had the spunk to bake pies, or cook up a nice pot of soup, or hang her wash out on the line. She had to stop taking in needy folks, because she couldn't even fix them a decent meal.

According to her doctor, her heart was getting worse, her eyesight was failing, and she had dropsy. In her weakest moments, she began to resign herself to the fact that the Lord was calling her. Yes, she thought, it must be time for old Auntie Clara to die. As cheerful as she was with visitors, deep inside she felt an emptiness. What had ever become of her precious Eliza Jane?

It was a puzzlement to Clara. After all, her Bible promised that, "What things soever ye desire, when ye pray, believe that ye receive them, and ye shall have them." There was nothing she had desired more than to see her daughter's face while she was still on God's earth.

Tuesday, February 14, 1882, was Valentine's Day, and Clara's name appeared in the "Notification of Mail" column of the paper. Letters were not delivered door-to-door. Instead, a list of names of those who needed to pick up mail at the post office was published in the *Rocky Mountain News*.

Everyone knew that Clara was shut in at home, so someone always picked up her mail and brought it to her. Of all the gifts of hearts and chocolates and flowers received that day, Clara's Valentine's Day surprise was the most memorable by far.

It was a letter from a woman who had once lived in Denver. She had since moved to Council Bluffs, Iowa, and was picking up her mail just the other day, she wrote. At the post office, she ran into a Mrs. Brewer, who'd come to pick up tickets for a play—a performance of *Uncle Tom's Cabin,* to be specific.

The postal clerk addressed Mrs. Brewer by the name of "Eliza Jane." Could this middle-aged woman standing right in front of her be Clara Brown's daughter? The woman spoke with Mrs. Brewer, who did not believe it was possible. She assumed that her mother had died in slavery years before. Still, they talked it over.

Mrs. Brewer had lived in Kentucky, she said, and when

she was ten or eleven, her whole family dressed up in their best clothes and were herded off to a slave auction. She remembered strangers forcing her to leave her family behind, and being carted off to a different farm, owned by the Covingtons. Later, she married a slave named Jeb from a neighboring farm. She became the mother of nine children, and stayed with the Covingtons for nearly twenty years. Jeb later died, and now her children were grown and all on their own.

Was Eliza Jane's mother named Clara? Eliza did not remember. Being "little-bitty" at the time, her mother was simply "mammy." What about a sister who drowned? That did it! Tears welled in Eliza's eyes, and she poured her heart out about her beloved twin, who drowned in the river.

Eliza Jane did not have the money to travel the six hundred miles to Denver to see whether Clara Brown was really her mammy. But if it was possible that her mother was still alive, and living in Colorado, she had to see her. Where could they meet? How soon could they meet? Eliza Jane was beside herself.

"When told that her mother was living in Denver, she became almost frantic in the desire to see her," the *Denver Republican* wrote that Saturday, after Clara shared the letter with a reporter. "And the letter was written in order to fully verify whether the relationship was true beyond the shadow of a doubt. Aunt Clara was unable to take the matter philosophically, and ever since the letter, has been crying for joy and thanking God for his goodness in restoring her child to her."

For Clara, the letter was the best medicine this side of heaven. She was suddenly back to her old self, and wild horses couldn't stop her from finding out the truth. She decided to go to Council Bluffs herself. She was well enough to travel, Clara told her doctor when he came to check on her.

The doctor wasn't quite as full of enthusiasm as Clara. He knew that many slaves had lived in Kentucky. Surely there had been other young slaves like Eliza who'd been bought by the Covington family, and other young children like Paulina Ann who had drowned in rivers or creeks. He had known Clara for years, and had seen her disappointed before. What if this woman was not Clara's daughter? One more disappointment could be too much for her frail heart.

Stubbornness kept Clara from listening. She was filled with joy, certain that this was her daughter. The Lord did not want her to die just yet. This was what she'd been praying for all these years—forty-six, to be exact.

The doctor, along with a few of Clara's longtime friends, was not so sure. It was possible that this woman in Council Bluffs was Clara's daughter. It was not, however, probable.

The reporter at the *Denver Republican*, enthralled by Clara's story, wanted to help. On Saturday, February 18, an article entitled "Story of Two Lives" gave readers Clara's life story in a nutshell, and declared with absolute certainty that

Aunt Clara had located her long-lost daughter at last. It ended this way:

The old auntie has
NO FUNDS TO PAY

Her passage, and she is waiting until her friends secure a pass or raise enough money to pay her fare. The old lady has had a half-fare ticket for several years, and if a full pass cannot be secured her friends will contribute enough to buy a railroad ticket. The old lady's face beams with delight as she anticipates meeting her daughter again, and says if her friends will buy a ticket for her she "can cook up enough to eat and take it along in a basket."

The case is one of

THE MOST REMARKABLE

Of the many sad stories that have been handed down from the days of slavery, and transportation should be provided for the old mother so that she can leave for Council Bluffs as soon as possible. It is a case worthy the consideration of the charitable people of Denver. If a pass cannot be secured, a contribution should be taken up, so that Aunt Clara may be able to go on her way rejoicing.

The news spread quickly through Denver, and Clara's friends and neighbors were so excited that as soon as one visitor left Clara's house, the next was knocking on her door. Aunt Clara just had to take that train trip to Iowa! They brought food for her trip, some clothes to spruce up her look, and offered spending money. The Union Pacific Railroad covered the remainder of her round-trip ticket to Council Bluffs. Friends, neighbors, and even strangers hoped to see her come home rejoicing, her Eliza Jane by her side.

Clara wasted no time. She answered the letter by telegram on February 17. She was coming to Iowa, she announced. She received a telegram in reply, confirming that she would meet Eliza Jane Brewer at the Eighth Street trolley stop in Council Bluffs, Iowa, on Saturday afternoon, March 4. Eighty-two-year-old Clara Brown packed up her things. She was going to fetch her little girl.

CHAPTER 21

One More Valley, One More Hill

On the morning of Friday, March 3, 1882, with picnic basket in hand, Clara boarded the eight-thirty Union Pacific train in Denver. The station was not the same as when she'd left for Kansas. It was brand new, and locals bragged it was the biggest building west of the Mississippi River. A gargantuan machine, the train screeched and steamed and chugged along the tracks on its way to Clara's first stop—Omaha, Nebraska.

"It's a miracle," people had told Clara when they'd heard about the letter. Now, riding past snowy fields and icy trees, Clara began to question whether it was, in fact, a miracle. It had been forty-six years! Liza would be in her late fifties. Would they even recognize each other? Worse yet, did Clara want this reunion too desperately? Perhaps she'd imagine this Iowa woman to be her daughter, even if she wasn't.

This massive new Denver Union station opened on June 1, 1881, and its tracks were always busy with narrow-gauge and standard train cars.

The train lumbered along the South Platte River, across the Great Plains, stopping now and then at small-town depots. As Clara passed the mills and farms and silos and cornhuskers and chicken coops, she rocked with the motion of the train, and remembered.

She remembered her baby, all alone on the auction block, trembling in her pink pinafore. She remembered the heart-wrenching separation that day, the darkness that had fallen when Eliza Jane was sold, loaded onto the wagon, and stolen from her life.

The train rumbled on to Grand Island, and patient Clara felt antsy as a child. She had not wanted to hurry when she had arrived in Denver in 1859; she had not wanted to hurry to get rich in Central City; but she wanted to hurry now. As fast as this train was moving, Clara ached for it to hurry faster.

Was Eliza really alive? If so, in the past forty-six years, she would have survived the separation from her mammy, the tortures of slavery, and the chaos and cruelty brought by emancipation. If this was Eliza, waiting on the other end, then the frail girl who never got over her twin sister's death could not be that frail, after all.

Clara's doctor had given her medication to calm her down. As darkness descended on the snowy fields, she took her pills. The train rocked and chugged on through the night, and on Saturday morning on the fourth of March, Clara arrived in Omaha, Nebraska.

With the conductor's help, she descended from the train. Now she would need to transfer to a streetcar, which would take her across the Missouri River to Council Bluffs, Iowa. Age had slowed Clara down like the Starvation Trail had slowed down those weary oxen so many long years ago. It wasn't like the old days when she was able to chop wood, jump the broom, and tramp across the Great Plains on her own sturdy two feet.

Everything was an ordeal—pulling on the coat and shawl, lugging the basket, maneuvering down the train car's narrow steps, and walking through the whistling, billowing steam into the station. Trying to decipher the "Exit" signs from the "Departures" and "Arrivals" and "Waiting Room" signs wasted precious time that Clara couldn't spare. As slow as her feet were, her rusty old heart was pushing her to hurry.

She found the streetcar stop and waited. The streetcar, or trolley, as it was also called, would take her to Eighth Street, Eliza Jane's street. It was late morning by the time Clara settled aboard the trolley. It was the size of a train car, with wooden benches for seats, and it traveled on rails like a train. But instead of running on noisy billowing steam, it was pulled by horses.

The streetcar screeched on the iron rails across the Aksarben Bridge over the Big Muddy—the Missouri River. Now they were in Council Bluffs, and Clara's heart raced. What was she doing, putting this enormous strain on herself? Hadn't she traveled enough of life's hills and valleys in her eighty-two years? Maybe she was just a crazy old lady, as some folks had whispered when they thought she couldn't hear them. A senile auntie, believing in the impossible.

The closer she got, the more Clara fidgeted and sighed and mumbled to herself. She got up and sat down all through the whole ride. Was this her stop? The conductor and the other passengers assured her it wasn't. They promised to tell her when to get off.

Every time the trolley slowed to a stop, there was Clara, jumping up from her seat, then sitting back down again. The passengers just shook their heads. When Clara finally arrived at Eighth Street, everyone turned. Nobody on that trolley was going to let this poor half-blind auntie miss her stop.

The horses trotted off, pulling the trolley behind. Clara stood alone beneath the dismal sky. Rain drizzled down, turning to sleet, and the streets were deep in puddles. What a gray, forgettable Saturday in March this was, for most people in Iowa!

Clara glanced around. The telegram had promised that Eliza Jane would be waiting when she arrived. The street was nearly empty, with only a few people hurrying to find someplace dry. But nobody was stopping for Clara. Used to disappointment, and used to faith beyond the visible, Clara stood right in her spot. She would wait.

She turned toward the sound of footsteps slapping through distant puddles. Clara squinted to make out a tall, blurry figure. Was it coming her way? With her poor eyesight, she could not tell if it was a man or woman, light or dark. But it did seem that the person was headed straight toward her. Could it be?

Clara began to pray out loud, rocking herself. Could her heart stand the joy if it was Eliza Jane? Could her heart stand the sorrow if it was not?

Clara saw the woman approaching now. Yes, it was a woman—nearly there, nearly standing right in front of Clara. She saw the long, drenched coat, and the caramel-smooth skin, the high cheekbones. Her gaze met the younger woman's gaze.

Clara's heart clutched. In a flash, beyond all doubt, Clara recognized the smile that was just like Richard's, and those sweet brown eyes that she would have known anywhere, no matter how much time went by.

"Mammy," Eliza Jane whispered. Reaching for her mother, Eliza took a step forward, lost her balance, and slipped to the ground, taking her mother right along with her. Clara did not care. She wrapped her own Eliza in her arms, and the two sat hugging in the muddy puddle, because nothing else mattered except that they were together.

How long did they sit in the wet, cold mud, unable to let go of each other? How long does a hug need to last to make up for forty-six years? Forty-six years of never holding your child in your arms? Or never feeling the safety of your mammy's love?

Forty-six years. More than five thousand miles. A thousand memories. A million tears. A lifetime of faith that, one day, despite all odds, this very moment would come to pass.

How long was that hug? Imagine.

CHAPTER 22

Carry Me Home

History is made every minute of every day by every human being. It is not just about wars and presidents and sweeping political revolutions. It is made and changed and colored by each person who lives in whatever time he or she is born to. Clara might not have expressed this, but deep in her bones, she knew it.

In her lifetime, she saw cities rise from the grasslands, train tracks crisscross the nation, electric lights replace smoky kerosene lamps. She saw the abolition of slavery and the near-extermination of entire Indian tribes. She saw leaders like Barney Ford and H. O. Wagoner, Benjamin Singleton, and Abraham Lincoln stand in the limelight, creating visible historic changes.

But Clara, with no big fanfare, changed history, too. Every down-and-out miner she took in soon thought twice before dismissing Negroes and Indians and Chinese and Mexicans as being in the way of white progress. Every former slave she nursed or housed or helped to find employment never again saw themselves as victimized or unloved or unable to sculpt their very own dream in a tough world. Every newspaper reader who learned about Clara's lifelong search for the daughter she never stopped loving had a little more faith in the invisible, in the improbable.

Clara did not journey home alone that March of 1882. According to the *Denver Tribune-Republican,* Eliza Jane came back with her to stay in Denver to live. She cared for her mammy in her last years, with the help of Clara's many friends. Eliza Jane had a chance to get to know her own mother at last: a woman of strength and tenacity, faith and humor. The many souls her mother had touched were there for her now, returning their love.

Clara was happy. Now growing older and weaker by the day, she knew she had accomplished all she'd been put on God's earth to do. Instead of deteriorating into a frail old woman, Clara aged like a proud African queen, or a Cherokee chief.

"She is a tall woman, very aged, yet she does not show the advance of years, save that she is toothless," a reporter wrote in June of 1885. "She has a remarkable face, with high cheekbones, a long, pointed nose, and very black eyes. Her cast of features is strong and almost classical, and the hair which curls above her temples is as white as the snow."

Although housebound most of the time now, she had a chance to show off those classical features in the fall of 1885. She was invited to a fancy Colorado Pioneer Society banquet. The mayor of Denver was celebrating the "Old Barnacles," and Clara was one of the special pioneers honored that evening.

On September 24, Eliza Jane helped her mammy get ready for the gala occasion. Though the fashions were suede gloves, ecru silk, black-and-white-striped satin, and Spanish lace, Clara dressed in her own style. She had never followed fashion trends, so why should she start now? She wore a calico dress with a white apron, and a colorful turban wrapped around her white hair. Her body was badly swollen from dropsy, so instead of shoes, Eliza tugged warm slippers onto her feet.

Too old to walk more than a few steps, Clara was carried to a buggy, and then into the St. James Hotel, by two friends. They seated her in an armchair at a prominent banquet table. As a reporter would say later, Clara had "the look of a high priestess" that night.

The whole banquet was a step back in time, with the original pioneers taking turns on stage to reminisce about wagon trains and salty grub, rattlesnake bites, and gold fever. Clara was especially honored as the only woman of color who was one of those official pioneers back in 1859.

Just one month later, friends and family gathered at Clara's bedside to pray—loyal friends she had known and loved throughout her years out west. Nobody was about to forget Aunt Clara at the time of her death. Nobody afterward would

AUNT CLARA BROWN.

Resolutions Adopted by the Colorado Pioneer Association—Mourning Her Loss.

The following resolutions in memory of Aunt Clara were adopted:

WHEREAS, Mrs. Clara Brown, a member of this Association and a pioneer in 1859, having passed to that land where sickness and suffering is not known, and

WHEREAS, The philanthropic disposition our dear friend showed by having smoothed the pillow and answered the appeal for help of many a poor sufferer in the days that tried the truest hearts, and

WHEREAS, We hold in grateful remembrance the kind old friend whose heart always responded to the cry of distress, and who, rising from the humble position of a slave to the angelic type of a noble woman, won our sympathy and commanded our respect; therefore be it

Resolved, That we sincerely mourn the loss of this noble woman whose many acts of benevolence made her presence like an angel's visit, and may Heaven amply reward her in the unknown land beyond the range.

Resolved, That a copy of these resolutions be spread upon the records and be published in all the city papers.

Pioneers J. Doldburg, Colonel J. M. Chivington and R. Sopris, comprised the Committee on Resolutions.

forget her faith and generosity and loving spirit, either.

Clara never wasted her time wondering: "Will I go hungry if I share my food with this starving miner?" Or "Will I go broke if I bring a group of lost souls to the Rocky Mountains and give them land and homes?"

No, she simply put one foot in front of the other and walked her path. She had always had faith enough to be led by her heart, and guided by God. Clara said:

"When I was a girl, I relied on His mercy, and He fetched me through."

Clara never complained. She was always quick to see the best in every person and every situation. She said:

"Oh, child, just stop and think how our Blessed Lord was crucified. Think how He suffered. My little sufferings was nothing, honey, and the Lord, He gave me strength to bear up under them. I can't complain."

Clara spoke her final word on the evening of Monday, the twenty-sixth of October, 1885. As if she were seeing her mother someplace down the golden road she was traveling, she cried out: "Mammy!"

Far from the rowdy boomtown gamblers, far from the honky-tonk saloons, Clara's circle of friends and family surrounded her bed and stood by her door and, like a choir of weeping angels, sang hymns outside her little white house in Denver. It was time for the Lord to carry sweet Aunt Clara Brown home at last.

The Research Trail

I first heard Clara's story in 1995 from a storyteller at the Boulder Public Library. I left the auditorium in tears. When weeks had passed and I found myself still thinking about Clara, I knew I had to write about her.

I began my research in the usual places: I searched the local libraries and surfed the Internet. What I found convinced me that Clara's amazing story was true. I expanded my research. Several people I talked to believed I would find little information about an ex-slave. Indeed, although Clara's spirit left a physical trail, her limited literacy did not allow her to leave behind writings or diaries. So I had to rely on the writings of others.

Wearing white gloves, I went through endless boxes of original manuscripts—diaries left by William Byers and Jacob

Adriance, records from the Colorado Society of Pioneers, and journals of pioneers who braved the Smoky Hill Trail in the spring of 1859. I went to courthouses in Central City, Denver, and Boulder to find records of Clara's land and mining purchases. A long-buried letter from a Kansas librarian, filed in a manuscript box in Denver, confirmed the existence of Becky Johnson. A private journal kept by a Central City neighbor of Clara's revealed old Auntie Clara's heart problem and consequent morphine treatment. The faded, handwritten entries in Reverend Adriance's diaries told me about the many prayer meetings held in Clara's two cabins.

As my journey continued, I fleshed out documented history with oral history. From an eighty-year-old woman in Leavenworth whose friend Lizzie had lived in Clara's day, I learned about "buggy" fertilizer and secret African American after-church gatherings. Occasionally, however, oral history led me astray. For instance, I learned of a tunnel beneath the Missouri River from a man who as a boy had once explored that tunnel. He followed it from the Missouri riverbank to the Kansas side, emerging from a Leavenworth sewer cover. He and others believed that this passageway had served as an Underground Railroad route. But my research revealed that if a tunnel is there (and many Leavenworthians have confirmed that it is), it was built later—too late to have been of use to escaping slaves. The technology needed to dig a tunnel beneath the wide Missouri did not exist in Clara's day. It's a great story, but it simply is not true.

Did Clara and Eliza, upon meeting, *really* slip in the mud on the streets of Council Bluffs and, soaked in rain and muck, keep hugging? Yes, they did. Different witnesses reported the sight in different ways, but the streets were puddle-muddy that March afternoon. We may never know who fell first, mother or daughter, taking the other one with her. We do know that there they sat, unwilling to let go.

Did Clara really walk more than six hundred miles across the Great Plains at age fifty-nine, never riding in the wagons? Clara herself, in one of only four published newspaper interviews I have found, said that she did. The diaries of argonauts who took the Smoky Hill Trail that same spring, although they do not refer directly to Clara, confirm that as hired help, she surely would have walked.

Did Clara sleep outside? Yes, my research tells me. But did she sleep outside every single night of her eight-week journey? I have taken the liberty of assuming that even the most bigoted argonaut did not want his cook, an old woman by nineteenth-century standards, to die of pneumonia from sleeping outside through dust storms, torrential cold rains, and a blizzard, conditions under which other hired help was given shelter. I have occasionally made other logical assumptions, keeping them to a bare minimum, including them only when their addition was essential to the flow of the story. All statements I have presented as fact have been confirmed from two reliable sources and, in most cases, from two primary sources.

Still, there is so much more detective work to do. With that, I extend a challenge to my readers. To those who have information about Clara, I hope you will get it out, dust it off, and share it with the world. Every detail, small as it may seem, is essential to drawing a clear profile of Aunt Clara Brown and her influence on those whose lives she touched. Where are her descendants, people I've not yet succeeded in tracking down? Do they have papers or oral history that shed more light on the incredible story of Aunt Clara? Who were her employers in St. Louis? I have not been able to confirm their names. In time, others may be able to fill in the blanks with whatever further documented information can be uncovered.

Clara's life was as integral to the expansion of the West as the lives of Buffalo Bill, Barney Ford, and William Byers. I hope that this book is first of many to establish Clara as one of the many pioneers who were not cowboys or gold miners or politicians but who had a major influence on the spirit of what is now the American West.

Selected Bibliography

Books

Brown, Robert L. *The Great Pikes Peak Gold Rush.* Caldwell, Idaho: Caxton Printers Ltd., 1985.

Bruyn, Kathleen. *Aunt Clara Brown: Story of a Black Pioneer.* Boulder: Pruett Press, 1978.

Christian, Charles M. *Black Saga.* New York: Houghton Mifflin Co., 1995.

Crossen, Forest. *Western Yesterdays.* 5 vols. Boulder: Boulder Publishing, Inc., 1965.

Currie, Steven. *Slavery.* San Diego: Greenhaven Press, 1999.

Katz, William Loren. *Black Pioneers: An Untold Story.* New York: Atheneum Books for Young Readers, 1999.

Noel, Thomas J. *The City and the Saloon*. Boulder: University Press of Colorado, 1996.

Schoolland, J. B. *Boulder in Perspective: From the Search for Gold to the Gold of Research*. Boulder: Johnson Printing Co., 1980.

Schultz, Duane. *Month of the Freezing Moon: The Sand Creek Massacre, November 1864*. New York: St. Martin's Press, 1990.

Shellenberger, Robert. *Wagons West: Trail Tales 1848*. Stockton, Calif.: Heritage West Books, 1991.

Smedley, William. *Across the Plains: An 1862 Journey from Omaha to Oregon*. Boulder: Johnson Printing Co., 1994.

Stewart, Elinore Pruitt. *Letters of a Woman Homesteader*. Lincoln: University of Nebraska Press, 1961.

Talmadge, Marian, and Iris Gilmore. *Barney Ford, Black Baron*. New York: Dodd, Mead & Co., 1973.

Letters and Diaries

Adriance, Jacob. Correspondence and diaries. Western Historical Collection files. Denver Public Library, Denver, Colo.

Bruyn, Katherine. Correspondence and research notes. Western Historical Collection files. Denver Public Library, Denver, Colo.

Byers, William. Correspondence and diaries. Western Historical Collection files. Denver Public Library, Denver, Colo.

Reitze, Henry. Autobiography. Copy in files of Colorado Historical Society, Denver, Colo.

Newspapers and Magazines

Colorado:
Colorado Magazine. 1927–1932.
Colorado Prospector. Various.
Daily Central City Register-Call. 1879–1880.
Denver Tribune-Republican. 1880s.
Rocky Mountain News. 1859–present.
Iowa:
Council Bluffs Nonpareil. 1880s.
Kansas:
Kansas City Journal of Commerce. 1859.
Leavenworth Times. 1859–1865.

Videos and Audio Recordings

The Black West: Dreamers. Prod. and dir. Nguzo Saba, 30 min. Beacon Films, 1982, videocassette.

Negash, Kay. *Two Colorado Pioneer Women.* Boulder: Sounds True Studios, 1991. Audiocassette.

Acknowledgments

In researching the story of Clara's life, I gained a humble appreciation for the time-consuming, painstaking work of archival preservation. I am grateful to the many people whose work makes it possible for you and me to turn delicate pages of personal journals, letters, and records that are 150 years old. Because of them, we can see faded penmanship that shows signs of fatigue or anger just from the angle of the handwriting, read lists of expenses jotted in the margins, and wonder if the stains on the pages came from sweat or coffee or tears. For all those involved in the process, I am grateful. I am grateful also to the following people who helped shed light on Clara's life:

In Colorado, Kay Negash, for her beautiful factual telling of Clara's story; Kathleen Bruyn, for her generosity in archiving extensive notes from her own 1960s research about

213

Clara's life; Ivy Joy Johnson at the Julesberg Visitors Center, for confirming historical and geographic details of Clara's Smoky Hill journey; Colleen Nunn and all the reference librarians at Denver Public Library's Western Historical Collection, who were endlessly helpful; Denver's Riverside Cemetery, where Clara is buried; the Carnegie Branch of the Boulder Public Library; and the Black American West Museum and Heritage Center in Denver.

In Kansas, Debra Dandridge of the University of Kansas in Lawrence, for her insight into Becky's and Clara's roles as servicewomen in pioneer communities; Ann Thompson and Dr. Richard Sheridan, for clearing up the Underground Railroad tunnel mystery; Mrs. Eleanor Jackson, Mr. John Calhoun, and volunteer Lula Dillon, who graciously met me in the Kansas Room of the Leavenworth Public Library to help me research; and librarian Jane Kelsey of the Kansas State Historical Society Collection Library/Archives.

In Nebraska and Iowa, Omaha's Union Pacific Railroad Museum; Kearney's Great Platte River Road Archway Monument, a wonderful multimedia adventure for families; and the librarians at the Council Bluffs Public Library.

In New York, Diane Landolf, for her terrific work on photo acquisitions; and my meticulous editor, Jim Thomas, who scoured the manuscript for questionable facts, patiently extended deadlines, and cheered me on when the going got rough. Painfully, he has made a better writer out of me.

And my husband, Rick Cleminson Keep, who for years

sacrificed vacations to join me instead on my journey through Colorado mining towns, Council Bluffs streets, Omaha train stations, Kansas libraries, and the hills and valleys of the Smoky Hill Trail.

Photos courtesy of:

Bettmann/CORBIS (p. 37).

Colorado State Archives (p. 205—Clara Brown commemorative stained-glass window in the Colorado State Capitol).

CORBIS (p. 24).

Denver Public Library, Western History Collection (cover, pp. 59, 77, 94, 101, 112, 129, 142, 148, 151, 182, 192, 195, 203).

Gilpin Historical Society (p. 134).

Richard Keep (pp. 8–9, 39, 68–69).

Library of Congress (p. 43).

North Wind Picture Archives (pp. 18, 32, 51, 176).

Index

Supreme Court, U.S., 45
Sweet Medicine, 121, 125

Taos Lightning, 117
Teller House, 173
Tennessee, 9, 36, 164–165, 166, 169,
    177, 178, 187
Thirteenth Amendment, 161, 164
trail grub, 84–85
Transylvania College, 17
Treasury, U.S., 118
Treaty of Horse Creek, 124

Uncle Tom's Cabin, 189
Underground Railroad, 49–50, 54,
    139
Union Pacific, 163, 169, 180, 186–187,
    193, 194
Union Sunday School, 115
Utah, 44
Utes, 125

Virginia, 7, 24, 25, 32, 164, 187

Wadsworth, Col., 61, 65, 66, 69, 70,
    71, 74, 79–80, 81, 83, 87, 88, 92
Wagoner, Henry O., 139, 174, 186, 200
Wagoner, Julia, 139
wagon-train plan, 65–71
Weekly Times, The, 57
Western Kansas Territory, 56
White Antelope, 150, 155
Wiggins, Scout, 105
Wilderness Road, 9, 42, 73, 143
Wootten, Dick, 117
Wyandotte, 175, 176, 182

Wynkoop, Maj. Edward, 150, 151,
    152, 153, 156
Wyoming, 157

About the Author

Linda Lowery was born and raised in Chicago. Her fascination with the American West began when she was little, listening to her grandfather's Wild West stories—in the early 1900s he had been a blacksmith in Montana and had shoed Buffalo Bill's horse! A *New York Times* best-selling author, Linda has written thirty-two books for children, several of which she has also illustrated in collaboration with her husband, Richard Keep. Linda and Richard reside in Colorado and central Mexico.

Relive history with Landmark Books®

Grades 2 and Up

MEET ABRAHAM LINCOLN

MEET BENJAMIN FRANKLIN

MEET CHRISTOPHER COLUMBUS

MEET GEORGE WASHINGTON

MEET THOMAS JEFFERSON

Illustrated

THE PILGRIMS AT PLYMOUTH

REVOLUTION! HOW THE REVOLUTIONARY WAR BEGAN

WESTWARD HO! THE STORY OF THE PIONEERS

Grades 4 and Up

MEET MARTIN LUTHER KING, JR.

ONE MORE VALLEY, ONE MORE HILL: THE STORY OF AUNT CLARA BROWN

THE PIONEERS GO WEST

Grades 6 and Up

AIN'T GONNA STUDY WAR NO MORE: THE STORY OF AMERICA'S
PEACE SEEKERS

THE AMERICAN REVOLUTION

THE DAY THE SKY FELL: A HISTORY OF TERRORISM

THE LANDING OF THE PILGRIMS

THERE COMES A TIME: THE STRUGGLE FOR CIVIL RIGHTS

THE WITCHCRAFT OF SALEM VILLAGE

3